A HISTORY OF THE
GREAT TRAINS

A HISTORY OF THE GREAT TRAINS

Chris Cook

Harcourt Brace Jovanovich
New York and London

Printed in Great Britain

LC 77–73046

ISBN 0–15–140930–7

First American edition

B C D E

The endpapers show five former Illinois
Central Titans at Congress Street Yard,
Chicago.

The title page illustration shows the
great suspension bridge over the
Niagara in 1859, built to connect the
United States and Canada by railroad.

Contents

The opening of the Stockton and Darlington Railway on 27 September 1825. George Stephenson's *Locomotion* heads the first steam train on any public railway in the world. It consisted of 21 waggons and *Experiment*, the first passenger coach.

1 Steam Comes of Age

The age of steam possesses its own very special magic. From the earliest engines like *Puffing Billy* to the glamour of the romantic Orient Express, steam locomotives and trains have captured the imagination of people the world over.

The Duke of Wellington was not an enthusiast. 'They allow the lower classes to move about,' he complained bitterly. In a sense the reactionary duke was right, for in the wake of steam came a great social and commercial revolution. The opening-up of continents, the rise of new industrial centres, the advent of new holiday resorts, relative ease of access to such faraway fabled cities as Constantinople and St Petersburg – all stemmed from the advent of the age of steam.

At the pinnacle of the steam era were the great trains that have become legendary – the Blue Train, the Orient Express, the Union Pacific, the Canadian Pacific, the Cornish Riviera, the Royal Scot, the Twentieth Century Limited. But this book is more than just the story of such famous expresses: it is concerned also with the nostalgia, adventure and achievement that they recall. Behind the great trains lay epic stories – of railway construction, for instance, particularly the great transcontinental routes, and of the development of ever faster and more powerful locomotives.

'Confound Romance'. . . . And all unseen
Romance brought up the nine-fifteen.

wrote Kipling, who knew a thing or two about railways. For anyone who still finds romance in the lost worlds of once familiar clouds of steam, one date marks the start of the new era – 27 September 1825, when the Stockton and Darlington Railway was opened. In 1830 there followed the first main line, the Liverpool and Manchester

1829.

GRAND COMPETITION
OF
LOCOMOTIVES
ON THE
LIVERPOOL & MANCHESTER RAILWAY.

STIPULATIONS & CONDITIONS

On which the Directors of the Liverpool and Manchester Railway offer a Premium of £500 for the most improved Locomotive Engine.

I.

The said Engine must "effectually consume its own smoke," according to the provisions of the Railway Act, 7th Geo. IV.

II.

The Engine, if it weighs Six Tons, must be capable of drawing after it, day by day, on a well-constructed Railway, on a level plane, a Train of Carriages of the gross weight of Twenty Tons, including the Tender and Water Tank, at the rate of Ten Miles per Hour, with a pressure of steam in the boiler not exceeding Fifty Pounds on the square inch.

III.

There must be Two Safety Valves, one of which must be completely out of the reach or control of the Engine-man, and neither of which must be fastened down while the Engine is working.

IV.

The Engine and Boiler must be supported on Springs, and rest on Six Wheels; and the height from the ground to the top of the Chimney must not exceed Fifteen Feet.

V.

The weight of the Machine, WITH ITS COMPLEMENT OF WATER in the Boiler, must, at most, not exceed Six Tons, and a Machine of less weight will be preferred if it draw AFTER it a PROPORTIONATE weight; and if the weight of the Engine, &c., do not exceed FIVE TONS, then the gross weight to be drawn need not exceed Fifteen Tons; and in that proportion for Machines of still smaller weight—provided that the Engine, &c., shall still be on six wheels, unless the weight (as above) be reduced to Four Tons and a Half, or under, in which case the Boiler, &c., may be placed on four wheels. And the Company shall be at liberty to put the Boiler, Fire Tube, Cylinders, &c., to the test of a pressure of water not exceeding 150 Pounds per square inch, without being answerable for any damage the Machine may receive in consequence.

VI.

There must be a Mercurial Gauge affixed to the Machine, with Index Rod, showing the Steam Pressure above 45 Pounds per square inch; and constructed to blow out a Pressure of 60 Pounds per inch.

VII.

The Engine to be delivered complete for trial, at the Liverpool end of the Railway, not later than the 1st of October next.

VIII.

The price of the Engine which may be accepted, not to exceed £550, delivered on the Railway; and any Engine not approved to be taken back by the Owner.

N.B.—The Railway Company will provide the ENGINE TENDER with a supply of Water and Fuel, for the experiment. The distance within the Rails is four feet eight inches and a half.

THE LOCOMOTIVE STEAM ENGINES,

WHICH COMPETED FOR THE PRIZE OF £500 OFFERED BY THE DIRECTORS OF THE LIVERPOOL AND MANCHESTER RAILWAY COMPANY.

DRAWN TO A SCALE ¼ INCH TO A FOOT.

THE "ROCKET" OF Mr. ROBT. STEPHENSON OF NEWCASTLE,

WHICH DRAWING A LOAD EQUIVALENT TO THREE TIMES ITS WEIGHT TRAVELLED AT THE RATE OF 12½ MILES AN HOUR, AND WITH A CARRIAGE & PASSENGERS AT THE RATE OF 24 MILES.
COST PER MILE FOR FUEL ABOUT THREE HALFPENCE.

THE "NOVELTY" OF MESSrs. BRAITHWAITE & ERRICSSON OF LONDON,

WHICH DRAWING A LOAD EQUIVALENT TO THREE TIMES ITS WEIGHT TRAVELLED AT THE RATE OF 20½ MILES AN HOUR, AND WITH A CARRIAGE & PASSENGERS AT THE RATE OF 32 MILES.
COST PER MILE FOR FUEL ABOUT ONE HALFPENNY.

THE "SANSPAREIL" OF Mr. HACKWORTH OF DARLINGTON,

WHICH DRAWING A LOAD EQUIVALENT TO THREE TIMES ITS WEIGHT TRAVELLED AT THE RATE OF 12½ MILES AN HOUR. COST FOR FUEL PER MILE ABOUT TWO PENCE.

Railway. Its famous Rainhill trials, won by George Stephenson's locomotive *Rocket*, were held the previous year.

From then on the building of trunk routes rapidly gained momentum. They were built between London and Southampton, London and Bristol (the Great Western Railway) and London and Birmingham. In 1837 the Grand Junction Railway was opened to link the London and Birmingham with the Liverpool and Manchester; a few years later the three lines amalgamated to form the London and North Western Railway. In 1844 the Midland Railway was formed by amalgamation of the North Midland, Midland Counties and Birmingham and Derby Junction Railways. Most of these railways were built to George Stephenson's 4 ft-8½ ins gauge. Only the Great Western, and associated lines, adopted the broad gauge of 7 ft 0¼ ins at the insistence of the great engineer Brunel. In 1846, after long controversy, it was decided that the 4 ft-8½ ins gauge should be standard and GWR lines were all, eventually, narrowed to conform.

The opening of the Britannia Bridge across the Menai Strait on 18 March 1850 completed the Irish Mail route from London to Holyhead. By the third quarter of the nineteenth century the network of trunk routes across the length and breadth of Britain was all but complete. The last main line – the Great Central route to Marylebone – came at the turn of the century.

From its beginnings in England the steam railway spread rapidly to other parts of the world. The first steam locomotive to run regularly in North America was the *Best Friend of Charleston* which started work on the South Carolina Railroad in 1829. There were already several railroads in North America on which vehicles were drawn by horses, and even without steam these were an improvement on dirt roads and on canals which, in the northern part of the country, were frozen all winter. Soon the *Best Friend of Charleston* was followed by other locomotives, and by 1832 they were running regularly over 23 miles of track in six states. The great need, however, was to open up the country west of the Allegheny Mountains and even farther afield, and by 1870 there were 50,000

Above The trial of speed between the experimental steam locomotive *Tom Thumb* and a horse-drawn carriage held in August 1830 on the Baltimore and Ohio Railroad, America's first long distance line.

Opposite The competition sponsored by the Liverpool and Manchester Railway in 1829 for a new and efficient steam locomotive to run on what proved to be the world's first main line. Stephenson's *Rocket* was an easy winner out of the three final competitors.

The opening in December 1835 of Germany's first railway, the *Ludwigsbahn*, between Nuremberg and Fürth. The train was powered by a Stephenson locomotive, *Der Adler*.

miles of track in use and the first transcontinental railroad had been completed to link the Atlantic and Pacific Oceans. Yet only in 1803 Thomas Jefferson had predicted that it would be 1000 years before territory west of the Mississippi would be settled.

In Britain, Europe, and the eastern part of the USA the railways connected existing towns and cities. But in the American west the railroad came first and settlement followed. That pattern was repeated elsewhere, notably in Canada, Australia and Africa. At the turn of the century Nairobi originated as a convenient spot for a construction camp for the railway being built from the coast to Uganda.

The main manufacturing centres for railway equipment, and the homes of many of the engineers who laid out the railways, were in the UK, the USA and the continent of Europe. Since styles of locomotives and rolling stock, and methods of operation, evolved separately in these areas, railways in other parts of the world came to reflect the practices of the country from which they originated. In Latin America, for instance, British practice prevailed in those countries where British capital financed the railways, and the influence of the USA was to be seen on the railways of other countries such as Chile, and Mexico and other central American countries. In Africa, railways tended to resemble those of whichever colonial power was involved.

The strange consequence has been that various types of

locomotive and other railway equipment, extinct in the countries where they were designed, have continued to be used in other countries far away. For example, steam locomotives in the USA have long been generally replaced by diesels, but USA-built steam locomotives are still running elsewhere – in Latin America, for instance, and even in communist China. Nowhere has this tendency been more marked than in India. Indian railways, despite a distinct local flavour, tend in many ways to be more British than those of Britain. British-style, and even British-built, steam locomotives continue to haul trains controlled by British-style semaphore signals and intending passengers still consult *Bradshaw* for the time of the next train to Poona Junction.

Though steam achieved its technical zenith after 1914, the real era of great trains lay in the halcyon days of the half-century before 1914. That was the era when legends were born and romance was unbridled. It saw the birth of the Orient Express, and a passenger boarding a train in London might have a ticket in his pocket for St Petersburg, Vienna or distant Constantinople. Passports were then unknown in the civilized world. Those years witnessed the crossing of continents by the iron horse, and the taming of wildernesses.

The arrival of the first locomotive at Indore, Central India, in 1875.

2 The Route to the West

Of the famous railway companies, the Great Western has a unique place in Britain's industrial history. The longest lived of the British main-line companies, it was incorporated in 1835 and survived until nationalization in 1948. During this long period it evolved a method of operation and a tradition of service by which its great trains are still fondly remembered today.

One man will always be associated with the Great Western: Isambard Kingdom Brunel. This engineer of genius conceived the vision of a great railway from London to Bristol – and on to Exeter, Plymouth and Penzance – as a single entity. It was built over beautiful bridges and through noble tunnels, on the 7-ft broad gauge. For this broad gauge a young locomotive superintendent, Daniel Gooch, built enormous express engines with driving wheels 8 ft in diameter, to provide faster travel than anything the world had yet seen.

The Great Western began as it was to go on. No railway company was to contribute more to the era of the great trains. The GWR was particularly distinguished by both style and ostentatiousness. Its later standard-gauge engines are well known. The Stars and Saints designed by Churchward were later developed by Collett when he produced his Castles and Kings. They were resplendently turned out in 'Swindon green' and lined in orange and black with copper-capped chimneys and brass safety valve covers. The company coat of arms, and the word 'Great Western' in gold lettering, were painted on the tenders of these famous express engines. Further variety and splendour were provided by the carriages, which were decked out in chocolate and cream. They too were decorated with the company coat of arms. Based on Paddington, its London terminus and headquarters, the company proceeded to build up its

Opposite Isambard Kingdom Brunel, architect of the Great Western Railway's broad gauge system. His bridges and tunnels still stand today as a monument to his engineering genius.

13

connections with the south-west and the midlands. Its first trunk line had been built between London and Bristol (hence its arms which consisted of these cities' shields placed side by side) and finished in 1841. From this base the GWR expanded into Devon and Cornwall. It also traced its lines around the coast of south Wales, linking this area with London. For the first time Swansea and Cardiff were connected with the metropolis by a quick and efficient means of transportation. The company later spread its activities into the Midlands, and operated the famous Cathedrals Express to Oxford, Worcester and Hereford. Birmingham Snow Hill was also to become a famous Great Western station. However, in 1948, the railways were nationalized by Attlee's Labour government and the GWR became Western Region. Yet for a time old traditions continued, the same engines were run, the familiar liveries were retained and the stations were operated as before.

Of all the expresses which the company ran, the Cornish Riviera stands out. The service was originally conceived in 1904. It was planned to run a new fast train from Paddington to Plymouth, some 246 miles, in 265 minutes by way of Bristol. Such a schedule involved a certain amount of rationalization of existing track. Originally the GWR route to the south-west had been somewhat circuitous and had earned the company the nickname 'Great Way Round'. In fact the directors started this popular service before the work was thoroughly completed: the first train left Paddington on 1 July at 10.10 am. *The Railway Magazine* caught the infectious enthusiasm surrounding the event and consequently ran a competition to discover a suitable name for this new train. As many as 1286 entries were received. From these James Inglis, General Manager at the time, chose the winning 'Riviera Express' which had been suggested by two entrants. Other names which were submitted included 'Cornish Riviera Limited' and 'The Royal Duchy Express', while a feature in the magazine, entitled 'British Locomotive Practice and Performance', jocularly referred to this express service as 'The Inglisman'. It is not certain whether the name 'Riviera Express' was ever used officially as the name by which the train is now known (Cornish Riviera) seems to have been adopted very early on. In the first timetables it was booked as being 'The Plymouth, Falmouth and Penzance Special'. To railwaymen the train has always been known as the 'Limited'.

The train originally consisted of six coaches including a fashionable dining-car, but as its popularity spread the company was forced to expand the service. During the train's first summer in operation the company was able to boost the length to seven or eight coaches and once to nine. Amazingly, the regular 4–4–0 engine was still able to pull this additional weight as far as Exeter without assistance. However, the heavier gradients past Newton Abbot necessitated the addition of a second engine. The train was particularly noted for its luxury and efficiency. The engines were

specially selected and highly polished for the occasion. The rolling stock was always of the highest quality and the service offered on the train was deliberately raised.

It was no accident that the opening of this new programme of express passenger services was followed with intense interest. For it was all part of a carefully prepared plan devised by the Great Western to increase its profits through the expansion of holiday and leisure travelling as distinct from purely business and commuter traffic. There was a planned programme of publicity suggesting Devon and Cornwall as idyllic resorts, even for winter holidays; the obvious comparison with the south of France was made and the economies and convenience of the English version were stressed. Rather spurious maps were drawn, showing a geographical similarity between Italy and the Cornish peninsula. Whether it was this publicity campaign which pulled in the passengers, or the very real attraction of this spectacular train and the beauty spots of its destination, it is difficult to say. Certainly the Cornish Riviera Express excited popular imagination.

An interesting but by no means unique feature of the run was the use of the slip coach. This was a device by which the train was able to deposit passengers at intermediate stations without losing any time. Carriages for particular stations were detached while the train was running at full speed. They then slowed down as they ran out of momentum and stopped in the station for which they were destined. Although the Cornish Riviera ran at speed non-stop from

Sultan, one of Daniel Gooch's huge express engines, with driving wheels 8 feet in diameter. He designed them specially to achieve high speeds on the Great Western broad gauge.

15

A contemporary engraving depicting the chaos caused by the change from standard to broad gauge at Gloucester, where passengers and luggage had to be transferred from one train to another.

Paddington to Plymouth, it also provided connections to Westbury and Weymouth by means of the slip coach. Further slip coaches allowed passengers to be delivered to Taunton, Minehead and Barnstaple, and to Exeter and the Torquay line. This was a good arrangement as the load was progressively lightened as the engine approached steeper and steeper gradients. For the 'riviera' resorts themselves there were self-contained corridor coaches, and only these were allowed to carry the coveted nameboard 'Cornish Riviera Express'. The others carried the name 'Paddington' followed by the names of the carriages' destinations. During the winter the train's length was reduced: only three compartment coaches and a restaurant car went to Penzance.

In its centenary year the Great Western made a special effort for all its services; and the Cornish Riviera received, not surprisingly, extra-special treatment. A new set of centenary coaches was built in 1935. They were designed to be particularly spacious and luxurious, and were produced with end doors only, featuring vestibule entrances and overhanging bow ends. They were also exceptionally wide, being 9 ft 7 ins across, which allowed the compartments to be unusually roomy. It was all due to Brunel that such spaciousness was possible. Unlike other railway engineers, he built his Great

One of the Great Western Railway's first pictorial posters advertising their services to the Ascot Race Meeting of June 1897.

Western lines with the 7-ft gauge. Standard gauge (4 ft 8½ ins), however, was given statutory blessing in 1846 and by 1892 all his broad-gauge lines had been converted. This left more space between the tracks on GWR lines than on any other lines. Unfortunately centenary coaches were limited in their routes by their width, and so tended to be confined to the express services to the west of England. They were turned out in traditional chocolate and cream livery, and presented a stunning sight when first used on this service in 1935, hauled out of Paddington by King class No. 6014 *King Henry VII*.

It was probably during the 1930s that the Cornish Riviera reached its high point. Holiday traffic was on the increase and had risen to almost unmanageable proportions. At summer weekends it was quite common for the train to be run with as many as six portions; fourteen coaches were by no means an unusual feature.

In 1923 the Great Western produced a small book entitled *The 10.30 Limited: Railway Book for Boys of All Ages*. It was a popular work which shows just how famous this train had become. It was written with an infectious enthusiasm for railways. The opening paragraph conveyed the atmosphere splendidly: 'The hands of the big three-faced clock at Paddington Station point to 10.15 as we arrive on Platform Number One. There is just time to take a cursory glance at the powerful locomotive which, with its train of twelve coaches, constitutes the most wonderful train in the world, the Cornish Riviera Express, familiarly known as 'The 10.30 Limited' – (10.30 was its departure time). Speaking of the engine *Princess Mary* the author notes, 'We have time to do little more than admire the grace and dignity of this "greyhound" of the iron track. As we see her this morning, she suggests the embodiment of concentrated power, and appears to be straining at the leash and anxious to stretch herself to full capacity.'

Another great express service introduced not long after the Limited was the Cheltenham Flyer. The train ran between Cheltenham and London via Swindon, and was inaugurated on 9 July 1923. It was first worked by No. 2915 *Saint Bartholomew*, a loco that continued to be selected for this coveted run. The service's frequently stressed selling point, offered to the punters and racegoers who regularly used the train, was that it was the 'fastest train in the world'. In 1932 the Great Western deliberately set out to cover the 77·3 miles between Paddington and Swindon in record time. The train had originally run at around 62 mph, completing the journey in about 75 minutes. At this stage it was the fastest stop-to-stop service operating in the British Isles. In 1929 its scheduled time was reduced to 70 minutes when its average speed was boosted to 66 mph. It was supreme in the world for speed, and other railway companies were anxious to crack this record. In 1931 the Canadian Pacific timed one of its crack engines at an average speed of 68·9 mph and took the record from British and Great Western hands.

In the following July the Cheltenham Flyer recaptured the record with a run timed at an average 69·2 mph. But to rub the message home hard, in September 1932 loco No. 5006 *Tregenna Castle* hauled a train of 190 tons in just 56 minutes 21 seconds between Paddington and Swindon. Its average speed, therefore, was 81·6 mph. Schedule time was worked up to an average of 71·4 mph to ensure that the service always stayed well ahead of its Canadian rivals. Unfortunately, soon after this the northern lines came into their own, and their streamlined engines came to dominate the rivalry for high speeds. To commemorate the Flyer's achievement and to help publicize passenger travel, the GWR produced in 1934 another booklet, called simply *Cheltenham Flyer*. It explained that the name of the express originated by chance; it was not of the company's making – the press christened the train. Certainly 'Swindon Flyer' would not have had the glamorous racing associations of Cheltenham. Tourists from all over the world included a trip on this train in their itineraries in the 1930s. One American visitor is reported to have made the run three times, arguing that 'it knocked travelling by air into a cocked hat', and adding that 'hitting London at 90 mph' appealed strongly to him. So great was the interest in this high-speed run that special fares had to be instituted so that numbers could be restricted by price.

Other famous express runs operated by the Great Western included the Bristolian and the Torbay Express. The Bristolian was first introduced in 1935 and ran from Paddington to Bristol non-stop. The two trains daily from Paddington at 10 am and back from Bristol, Temple Meads, at 4.30 pm were operated by the same crews based at Old Oak Common Shed, London. The most powerful Great Western engines, Collett's King class, a development of the more numerous Castles, were used in an attempt to rival the high-speed runs now being made by the London and North-Eastern Railway. Unfortunately they were not able to match the Silver Jubilee express, and after a short time modified Castles replaced the Kings with great success, keeping up the scheduled 72 mph for the 82 miles between London and Bristol.

The Bristolian evolved from the Cheltenham Flyer, and the success of the Cornish Riviera to the south-west encouraged an expansion of services in that area. The section of the train that was slipped at Exeter came to be known as the 11.50 Torquay Diner.

It would be unfair to conclude this section of railway history without due attention to those engines which made the Great Western famous. Anyone who studies pictures of the company's engines from the Bulldogs through to the Kings will spot a continuity in design, a certain quality which can only be called 'Great Western'. The pattern was originally set by George Jackson Churchward, chief mechanical engineer to the company from 1902 to 1921. He was responsible for the development of the Stars and Saints, new and more powerful express engines with the looks of

The excitement and bustle of Paddington Station, the London terminus of the Great Western Railway, captured by the Victorian painter Charles Frith. On the left departing schoolboys make their farewells, in the centre a cab driver argues with a bewildered foreigner, while, to the right of the bridal party, two Bow Street runners arrest a suspect.

Above The Torbay Express, hauled by the Castle class *Swordfish*, travels along the magnificent coastline overlooking Torbay, South Devon.

Opposite above The Cornish Riviera, the Great Western's most famous express service, leaves Paddington Station, London headed by one of Collett's great King class engines *King Richard III*.

Opposite below Wintry conditions for The Red Dragon Express en route from London to Carmarthen, South Wales.

the later Collett classics. They had the characteristic taper boiler and 4–6–0 wheel arrangement. Collett, his successor, realized that progress required faster and more powerful engines; consequently he took these basic designs and modified them technically and stylistically to produce the now famous Kings, Castles, Manors, Halls and Granges. The Kings, originally to be called Cathedrals, were the ultimate development of this breed of loco – with four cylinders and a 4–6–0 arrangement they were the biggest and most powerful. To gain further publicity it was decided to send the first of their number to the Baltimore and Ohio Railroad centenary celebrations in America in 1927. This led to the change of name. For an engine representing Great Britain, the obvious name of *King George V* was adopted for No. 6000. The name 'King' fitted admirably with the sentiments of the designers, suggesting might and majesty. The King class was, however, basically a development of Churchward's principles as embodied in the Star class. Bigger cylinders and higher boiler pressures combined with smaller coupled wheels gave this engine a final tractive effort of 40,300 lb, far in advance of any other British locomotive of the time. The King was the ultimate development of Churchward's loco design; weight restrictions prevented any further extension.

The Cambrian Coast Express from Aberystwyth to London on the mid-Wales coast, double headed near the summit of Talerddigg Bank.

Opposite King George V, the most famous of Collett's Great Western King class on a special run in 1972.

Right Clun Castle built in 1950 to Collett's design of the 1920s. It was later modified and in this form represents the final phase of the powerful Castle class locomotives.

3 Race to the North

A series of mergers in 1923 produced two large and powerful railway companies which competed for passenger traffic between London and Scotland – competition which led to higher and higher speeds and culminated in the world speed record for steam locomotives which remains unbroken. The companies were the London, Midland and Scottish Railway and the London and North-Eastern Railway. The route of the former ran from Euston Station northwards via Crewe and Carlisle – the 'west coast route'; that of the latter from King's Cross Station by way of York and Newcastle – the 'east coast route'. The LMS route included the climbs over Shap and Beattock summits; the LNER route was relatively level.

These two routes were no strangers to competitive running. Back in 1888, when there were two companies involved in the west coast route (London and North Western, and Caledonian) and three on the east coast (Great Northern, North Eastern, and North British), there had been an outbreak of 'racing'. Schedules on each route were alternately speeded up several times over a period of a few months, and the times from London to Edinburgh (10 hours west coast and 9 hours east coast) were both eventually reduced by one hour. Finally it was agreed that the schedule should be 8½ hours by either route. There was more racing in 1895, with Aberdeen as the goal – the opening of the bridge across the Firth of Forth had enabled the east coast route to compete. The two routes met at Kinnaber Junction for the final few miles to Aberdeen, and there were heroic scenes in the dawn when trains which had raced independently through the night over 500 miles came at last into one another's view – and one of them had to be held by signals for the other to speed through the junction ahead of it.

An excessive-speed accident at Preston in the early part of 1896

Opposite The early rivalry between the east and west coast routes from London to Scotland reflected in a poster issued in about 1895 advertising the east coast service to Scottish holiday resorts.

Overleaf:
Left above A Stanier Black Five hauls a London to Glasgow overnight express up Shap Bank, Cumbria, one of the steepest gradients on the LMS route to the North.

Left below Leander, another famous LMS Stanier locomotive, photographed in its restored livery at York Station in 1975.

Right The *Flying Scotsman* No. 4472, probably the most famous locomotive in the world. One of Sir Nigel Gresley's Pacifics, it was designed specifically for fast runs on the LNER route to the North. It is now preserved and is seen here at Sellafield, Cumbria, in 1974.

27

put an end to the public taste for racing, and thereafter for over thirty years trains on both routes ran to agreed schedules which were adequate, but not exceptionally fast. After the mergers there was a settling-down period for the new companies, followed by the industrial troubles of 1926 – the General Strike, which of course included a coal strike. It was not until 1927 that things started to happen again.

First the LMS, in response to Collett's Castles on the Great Western and Gresley's Pacifics on the LNER, decided to introduce the famous 4–6–0 Royal Scot class engines to run its route to Glasgow and Edinburgh. To speed up this run the 10 am from Euston to Scotland was retimed from July 1927 to challenge the east coast route's Flying Scotsman. The train was now scheduled to run non-stop from Euston to Glasgow as far as passengers were concerned. Although one stop was made to change engines and another at Symington to split the train into its Edinburgh and Glasgow sections. At first the train, consisting of fifteen coaches making up a total load of 420 tons for the loco, was double headed by a Claughton class 4–6–0 and a George the Fifth 4–4–0. Euston to Carnforth was a non-stop run of 236 miles which was covered in record time by these two engines in the space of 265 minutes, at an average speed of 53·3 mph. The first Royal Scot class locos were delivered by their designers and builders, North British Locomotive Company, from August 1927 onwards, and their introduction into this service was timed for 26 September 1927. It was a daring enterprise to put new and really untried engines on a prestige run. There was also the prospect of a tough winter ahead. This lengthy run was not as smooth as those on the Great Western, and trains had several difficult gradients to tackle, notably Shap and Beattock banks.

The whole enterprise was given massive publicity in an effort to swing passengers away from the east coast route, and the train was named the Royal Scot. To popularize the service in Scotland, the first twenty-five engines completed were all later given regimental names, many of which were Scottish, such as *Scottish Borderer* and *Cameron Highlander*. Other regiments selected included those situated along the route in England and included *South Lancashire*, and *The Prince of Wales' Volunteers*. They were not handsome engines in the way that Castles and LNER Pacifics were, but nevertheless had a certain style and were particularly distinguished by their tapered boiler and large smokebox with a tiny chimney. The engines which were selected to work the west coast route were specially maintained and were given the best crews to ensure that good times were regularly returned. However, the class when used on other northern expresses was neither so reliable nor so impressive. The service as a whole deteriorated. The 'non-stop' running of the Royal Scot lasted for one winter alone, after which a stop at Crewe was incorporated. In addition in 1928 the separate dining-car laid on for the Edinburgh portion of the train was discontinued and the total weight of the stock was also reduced to around 400 tons. The older Claughton class 4–6–0s could still on occasions return performances as good as, if not better than, the newer Royal Scot class. Although initial tests with dynamometer cars showed that they seemed to combine sufficient power with low coal consumption, it was now becoming clear that these engines were simply not big enough to cope with this difficult and long run if they wished to compete with Gresley's powerful and speedy Pacifics. Investigation showed that improved piston rings would noticeably improve their performance, and this began to show effect around 1931. With this improvement in their efficiency they were able occasionally to match their 4–6–2 successors on the run. They continued to be popular engines, a fact confirmed by their continued construction and impressive naming ceremonies. Regiments honoured in this way often brought their bands along to the unveiling ceremony and presented a coat of arms to go with the name-plate on the engine. The Black Watch, for example, paraded their pipers when their engine (No. 6102) was named at Glasgow Central Station on 15 October 1930. Only one of their class, No. 6114 *Coldstream Guardsman*, was ever involved in a serious accident while engaged on the Royal Scot run. This was a derailment at Leighton Buzzard. It took place on a Sunday – 22 March 1931 – when maintenance work was being undertaken on the fast down line from Euston. Signs were displayed where the train had to cross over on to the slow line to avoid the obstruction, and indicated a speed restriction of 20 mph. The driver chose to ignore them and raced over the crossover at a dangerous 60 mph. The loco was sent flying off the rails and overturned, killing the driver and fireman, three passengers in the leading coaches, and one of the dining-car staff. Because the driver had a good record it was suggested that it was not he who had ignored all these warnings but that it was the locomotive which had failed. It was argued that smoke from the chimney might have swept down to block the driver's vision; this was a failing of the class and subsequently all engines in it were fitted with smoke deflector plates.

However, as the LNER continued to return better and better times, increased pressure was put upon W. A. Stanier, who had come from the GWR to be chief mechanical engineer of the LMS, to produce a new Pacific-type engine to handle heavy, fast express trains to the north. He was in fact ordered in 1932 to produce six new types of engine to cover all the requirements of railway haulage, but priority was given to the Pacifics which were required to boost the company's tattered prestige. Stanier looked to the Great Western in part for inspiration and the first two of his Pacifics were completed at Crewe in the summer of 1933. The first was No. 6200 *The Princess Royal*, which with subsequent locomotives formed the Princess Royal class.

Because it was designed to run some 400 miles between Glasgow

A poster produced by the LNER to mark the inauguration of the fast Silver Jubilee service between London and Newcastle in 1935.

and London, a locomotive of this class was in some senses difficult to work. It was fitted with a large boiler and an exceptionally large firegrate, and firemen used to the smaller Royal Scots were at first intimidated by this engine. New techniques took some time to learn. Otherwise, the engines proved to be smooth, powerful and fast.

In the meantime schedules on the Anglo-Scottish run had been jacked up; from May 1932 the Midday Scot express was expected to run between Euston and Rugby in 88 minutes. But it was soon discovered that the new engines were not consistent over 400 miles and would need some serious modification. A new boiler, redesigned superheater and altered firebox produced a fine steaming engine. From the winter of 1935 onwards there were sufficient numbers of them to run the regular expresses to Scotland. These new engines were easily capable of taking loads of 500 tons on long and fast runs. The late spring of 1936 witnessed an important acceleration in the timing of the Midday Scot. Its overall time was now down to $7\frac{1}{2}$ hours for the 402 miles from Euston to Glasgow.

One of the best known of the early Stanier Pacifics was *Princess Elizabeth*, No. 6201. She was the engine chosen for a very special task in November 1936, to run non-stop between Euston and Glasgow at record speed. At the heart of this run was the east coast–west coast rivalry. From 1935 onwards the LNER had secured a great deal of publicity and hence passenger revenue from their new streamlined train, the Silver Jubilee, running between London and Newcastle, which reached speeds of over 100 mph. When the LNER announced in 1936 that it was going to introduce a streamlined flyer between London and Edinburgh, taking only 6 hours, the LMS decided to reply with a similar 6-hour run between Euston and Glasgow up the west coast route. With a load nearly equivalent to the Silver Jubilee, a round trip from Euston to Glasgow was planned taking 6 hours each way. The run was made on 16 November 1936 and was a tremendous success. The train reached Glasgow in 5 hours $53\frac{3}{4}$ minutes with a load of 225 tons, and the return was made even faster in only 5 hours $44\frac{1}{2}$ minutes.

After this speed trial the decision was made to go ahead with a regular, scheduled high-speed service from 1937 onwards. It was decided that a modified Princess Royal class should be built in preparation for this new service and that the locomotives should be streamlined, but look distinct from their LNER rivals. This fresh design was called the Princess Coronation class. The design's aerodynamic casing presented a striking appearance. But then after all the build-up the company decided that the new, scheduled midday run would be set at $6\frac{1}{2}$ and not 6 hours after all, destroying the element of competition altogether. The Coronation Scot, as it was called, did nevertheless make several 100-mph-plus runs. One was on 9 June 1937, when the driver of the engine *Coronation*, No. 6220, was instructed to break the LNER's speed record which then stood at 113 mph. Despite some extremely fast and almost disastrous

The Royal Scot steaming up Beattock Bank, Dumfriesshire, on the LMS route to the North.

driving, the heroic attempt narrowly failed as the engine never exceeded 112½ mph.

The leader and eventual unchallenged winner of the steam speed race to the north was the LNER under the expert guidance of its chief mechanical engineer, Sir Nigel Gresley. His first achievement in express engine design was the creation of the new Pacific class subsequently made famous by the now preserved locomotive *Flying Scotsman*. These locomotives were originally designed in 1922 for long, fast runs out of King's Cross. In 1923 the first of Collett's Castles appeared, and it was a nice coincidence that two famous engines appeared side by side at the 1924 Empire Exhibition at Wembley; No. 4073 *Caerphilly Castle* was placed alongside the specially named *Flying Scotsman*, No. 4472. At this stage rivalry for fast speeds was most intense between the LNER and the GWR, and the record was held by the latter in its runs to the south-west. In 1928 it was decided to publicize a new prestige LNER service; a non-stop train from King's Cross to Edinburgh to be called The Flying Scotsman. It began on 1 May, hauled by the engine of the same name. The time for the run, 8½ hours, was not set particularly high, but emphasis was laid on punctuality. However, the next improvement in LNER timekeeping was to come with Gresley's development of the Pacific type and the production of the streamlined A4 class locomotives, which were to break all known records.

The mid-1930s were the time when streamlining techniques were first being taken seriously. The idea was that a suitably shaped steel casing fitted over the engine would increase its efficiency by as much as forty per cent by reducing wind resistance. The image of the 'streamlined' train also suggested modernity and progress; the streamlined engine had a new, eye-catching look which the LNER considered would attract passengers. On 27 September 1935 Gresley's first streamlined engine *Silver Link*, No. 2509, emerged on

34

her first trial run; with this completed, the Silver Jubilee service between King's Cross and Newcastle was initiated. Speeds of 100 mph plus were a regular feature of the run; and, almost more remarkable, the Silver Link succeeded in running the journey there and back, some 536 miles, every day for the first two weeks of the service without any technical hitches. Gresley was knighted that year for his services to railway design. On one of its early trial runs A4 No. 2512 *Silver Fox* set up a new world speed record of 113 mph on 27 August 1936. This speed has remained the record for a train carrying fare-paying passengers on a scheduled service.

Encouraged by its success with the Silver Jubilee, the LNER decided to expand the scope of its fast, prestige services. In July 1937 it put on the Coronation streamlined express, scheduled to run from King's Cross to Edinburgh in 6 hours. As soon as the A4s were produced in sufficient numbers other expresses, including the Flying Scotsman, were provided with them. The most famous A4 of all was No. 4468 *Mallard*. On 3 July 1938 she steamed at 126 mph with a seven-coach train for 5 miles down Stoke bank on a test run, and in doing so secured the world steam speed record; it has never been beaten. *Mallard* is now preserved, quite appropriately in LNER colours, in the National Railway Museum, York.

The era of the high-speed steam train in Britain was regrettably short, and came to an abrupt end with the outbreak of war in 1939. Speeds of all trains were immediately reduced, and high-speed fliers disappeared from the timetables altogether. They were replaced by the crowded, slow, dirty and uncomfortable trains of the 1940s which in turn gave way to the inevitably less crowded, equally dirty and uncomfortable, and only a little faster trains of the 1950s. Not for twenty-five years or so, until the 1960s – by which time diesel and electric power had largely replaced steam – did the performance of British express trains start regularly to exceed that of the 1930s.

An excited crowd gathers at King's Cross Station to speed the Flying Scotsman on its non-stop run to Edinburgh in May 1928.

One of Sir Nigel Gresley's distinctive streamlined A4 Pacifics heads the Flying Scotsman at King's Cross in 1939.

Victoria Station, London in 1910. The importance of this station steadily increased as it became the gateway to the continent of Europe.

4 Pullmans in the South

The word Pullman has become synonymous with luxury travel: it is now regularly applied to motor coaches, which have usurped a railway term. Pullman cars, luxury vehicles, were the brainchild of George M. Pullman in the USA. Starting in the 1860s, his company built and provided the cars which many railroads incorporated into their trains. His business expanded into England, at the invitation of the Midland Railway, in 1874. The idea quickly spread, and Pullman cars in various forms and on various routes have been a feature of British railways ever since. Particularly distinctive have been those expresses composed entirely of Pullmans, or almost so; and perhaps the most famous of these was the Golden Arrow. The service connected London and Paris; the separate Pullman trains in England and France were linked by a Channel ferry. It reached its zenith during the years just before and just after the second world war; during the latter period the Golden Arrow was perhaps a symbol of the return of normality, of the resumption of peacetime links with the continent after the isolation of wartime. The rich and the famous travelled by the Golden Arrow. In London two warnings, one five minutes before departure and another one minute before, in English and French, were needed to clear admirers and friends from the train before it left. In France the Golden Arrow connected with the Blue Train for travellers going on to the Riviera.

The origins of the Golden Arrow can be traced back to the early expansion of English Pullman services. With its heavy tourist traffic to the south coast resorts the London, Brighton and South Coast Railway soon realized the attraction of these ostentatious coaches. It ran its first Pullman car in 1875 and its first train composed entirely of Pullmans in 1881. The idea of running these coaches in a service to the continent was tried as early as 1882, when the London, Chatham and Dover Railway Company ran the Pullman carriage *Jupiter* on its line to Dover; it was not, however, a success. In 1889 the notion was revived, with the International Exhibition in Paris in mind. Travellers to this famous show provided sufficient incentive for the LC and D and the South Eastern Railways to provide special luxury expresses; the actual carriages were provided by the European *Wagons-Lits* company. But even these additional passengers were not sufficient to justify this extra expense, and the service was discontinued four years after its inception.

Meanwhile the LBSCR had had better fortune with its service of Pullman boat-trains between Victoria Station and Newhaven. Its success provided a fillip for the other railway companies in the south-east, and in 1910 the South Eastern and Chatham Railway started operating Pullmans to the coastal ports. While all this was going on in England, the French were developing luxury services to their Channel ports. The first world war, however, temporarily interrupted the development of these services. Hence it was not until after the grouping of 1923 which resulted in the formation of the Southern Railway that these schemes started to be taken seriously again.

The foundations for the Golden Arrow, or *Flèche d'Or* as it was known in French, were laid in November 1924 when the Southern Railway opened its new Pullman service from Victoria to Dover. The first train consisted of seven Pullman cars with one or two first-class carriages and a brake van. It left Victoria at 10.50 am and arrived at Dover at 12.32. The train was drawn by the new King Arthur class engines, of 4–6–0 wheel arrangement. In 1926, after lengthy discussions with the Northern Railway of France, it was proposed to institute a through service from Victoria to Paris via Calais and Dover. To publicize the initiation of this famous service a special run was made on 11 September 1926 between Paris and Calais for journalists and railwaymen themselves. To emphasize Anglo-French co-operation, the carriages for the new service were specially constructed in England, and the whole train was hauled by a Nord Breville Super Pacific loco. Though they looked from the outside to be the same as regular Pullman carriages, they were in fact larger and slightly more luxurious. Both the saloon and coupé cars were finished in wood veneer with marquetry decoration, and no more than three carriages ever had the same interior design. They were all fitted throughout with electric lights. Special kitchen compartments were provided in those carriages which were designed as diners as well. Ten of these new carriages were laid on for this inaugural run. A regular service between Paris and Calais was instituted the next day to connect with the Isle of Thanet ferry, and was called the *Flèche d'Or*. The French authorities conceded that customs searches and passport checking could be undertaken on the train itself, saving passengers valuable time.

Back on English soil, the Southern Railway took steps to smarten up its end of the journey to the Channel ports. They renamed the service to Dover the Continental Express; although it was generally billed as an all-Pullman express, it did in fact often contain regular Southern stock, sometimes third-class. It was scheduled to leave Victoria at 10.45 am and arrive at Dover Marine at 12.23 pm. On reaching Calais by the ferry, travellers were in time to catch the *Flèche d'Or* at 2.10 pm and arrived in Paris at the *Gare du Nord* at 5.40 pm. In addition to these timetable and stock improvements effected by the Southern, there were changes in route. Much of the line was straightened and relaid to permit a smooth efficient run to the south. Because there had been so many railway companies operating to the south coast from London there existed a whole host of alternative routes to Dover, and the revitalized Southern Railway was able to take advantage of them. Evidence of their complexity can be seen in the fact that the Germans were unable to destroy the links between the Channel ports and London during the second world war, despite their concerted heavy bombing raids.

It was not until 15 May 1929, however, that this service between Victoria and Dover was renamed the Golden Arrow. The ordinary green Southern coaches were now absent, leaving the more colourful chocolate and cream of the Pullman cars with their individual names and Pullman crest on either side. The schedule was also modified and the departure time was put back to 11 am. Special arrangements were concluded with British customs to speed up the proceedings at Dover. A new ferry was commissioned for the passengers and was christened *Canterbury*. Although the new boat was capable of taking nearly 2000 passengers, it was decided to carry no more than 250–300 so as to preserve a luxurious and leisured atmosphere; it featured amongst its facilities a palm court.

In July 1930 the British section of the train was provided with eight rebuilt Pullman cars to replace some older and more antiquated carriages. The complete fare for this first-class travel between the capitals of England and France was £5. It was unfortunate that the directors of the Southern and Northern Railway Companies chose this period to float their new luxury service, for the 1930s witnessed a world slump and trade depression. Few people could afford to travel on this extravagant service and the number of passengers declined. The number of coaches had to be reduced and in May 1931 the scope of the service was cut back. The number of people using the formerly exclusive *Canterbury* was increased by cutting the cost and reducing the facilities. Second-class passengers as well as regular first-class travellers were permitted on board in 1932. The fare for the Golden Arrow was reduced by seven shillings and sixpence to compensate for the loss in services, and to encourage more people to travel on it. In France,

the *Flèche d'Or* underwent change. Second-class Pullman coaches were introduced, and sleeping cars which were part of the Calais-Mediterranean Express, the Rome Express and the Simplon-Orient Express were incorporated for economy's sake. In England second-class Pullmans were not introduced until 1949 on the Golden Arrow, though after 1932 regular Southern second-class coaches were included in the train, so that by 1939 there were usually only four Pullman cars on the whole train. Of course, the outbreak of war in 1939 meant the suspension of services until hostilities were over. The war also destroyed many of these impressive coaches and several cross-Channel ferries were lost. It was not until 15 October 1946 that the Golden Arrow service started again from Victoria on its traditional run. The inaugural train was aptly headed by the Bulleid Merchant Navy class 4–6–2 *Channel Packet*. The *Canterbury* had been released from war service and, with her guns removed, was ready to get back to her old job of conveying railway passengers.

The Southern Railway initially had the problem of stocking the reborn service. Post-war shortages meant that it was virtually impossible to build a whole set of new carriages. The old Pullmans were cleaned and overhauled ready for the run. The one development was the introduction of a bar-carriage to serve drinks between Victoria and Dover; this carriage was aptly christened the Trianon Bar. Nine reconditioned coaches were provided for the first run. Another innovation was the painting of the words 'Golden Arrow' on the sides of the carriages; later, however, because the carriages were occasionally used on other runs, the painted lettering was replaced by removable boards. The departure time was brought back to 10 am and the service was running again.

As air travel began to draw away passengers in the late forties and early fifties, it became necessary to reduce the level of services on the Golden Arrow. October 1949 saw the introduction of second-class Pullmans. But the new Bulleid Merchant Navy class Pacifics which now hauled the Golden Arrow were specially decorated for

The Golden Arrow being hauled out of Folkestone Harbour Station by two tank engines, prior to being taken over by a powerful Pacific engine for the run to London – a photograph taken in the early 1960s when the distinctive chocolate and cream Pullman coaches formed only part of the service.

the run; attached to the front of the engine was a disc bearing the words 'Golden Arrow' with an arrow running diagonally across it. The British and French flags were attached to the buffer, and along each side of the boiler was a large gold arrow pointing in the direction of travel. The French locomotives had a similar, though simpler, motif on their fronts as well. Another innovation on the train was a loudspeaker system, as on the competing aircraft, to announce details of the journey and customs regulations.

Timings, however, in 1946 were not good. The train took 8 hours 45 minutes to complete the journey between London and Paris, as compared with $6\frac{1}{2}$ hours in 1914. Delays were still being caused by wartime damage to track in both countries. The schedule was progressively reduced to 6 hours 35 minutes by the 1950s, partly because of the introduction of electric engines. A complete electric run from Victoria to Dover was inaugurated on 12 June 1961. The last steam engine to pull this historic train had been the West Country class 4–6–2, No. 34100 *Appledore*, the day before.

This run ended thirty-two years of steam express running for the Golden Arrow in England, interrupted only by the two world wars. These mighty Pacific engines were then replaced with the British Railways 71 class electric locomotives. These continued, though, to carry the Golden Arrow nameplate mounted on the front of the cab. In France electrification also proceeded apace. From 1960 onwards the *Flèche d'Or* was hauled by an electric locomotive from Paris to Amiens, and from Amiens to Calais by a steam locomotive, but in 1969 the latter was finally replaced by a diesel engine.

From the introduction of second-class Pullman coaches the Golden Arrow may be considered to have gone into a decline. It received some support in 1951, nevertheless, when the Festival of Britain was attracting foreign visitors from the continent. Most of the stock was then replaced, with some brand-new Pullmans and some refurbished stock. Yet by 1954 it was clear that the Golden

Arrow was still losing its attraction and Southern Region was again slipping in the conspicuous green coaches. In May 1965 it officially became part-Pullman only, with just four of the chocolate and cream carriages. Some said that the 'golden way' had now become the 'gold-plated way'. In France, the reductions in service were more drastic still; from 1946 the train was only part-Pullman with regular SNCF stock. By the 1960s the *Flèche d'Or* was usually only featuring one or two Pullman carriages, with meals being provided in the regular restaurant car. In December 1967 facilities were reduced still further.

Since then the Golden Arrow Pullman Service has been withdrawn entirely. A seven-hour London–Paris journey by train, ship and train, however luxurious, was no match for an air journey of fifty minutes, even allowing for lengthy and inconvenient bus journeys to and from airports.

Besides relying upon suburban and freight traffic for its revenues, the Southern Railway, and the various companies from which it was formed in 1923, was based on holiday travellers. With its main London termini at Victoria and Waterloo, its links with the west and the south coast, this railway was amply provided to deal with this traffic. In addition, holidaymakers coming south from the midlands were naturally drawn into London, centre of the English railway system, where they could transfer on to the Southern by means of the Underground initially designed to link up London's major railway termini. It is not surprising, therefore, that the Southern Railway became famous for its 'Belles'. Running almost due south was the Brighton Belle, composed entirely of Pullman cars. It was followed in 1931 by the institution of the Bournemouth Belle, first running on Sundays only between Waterloo and Bournemouth West, later on weekdays also in summer, and after 1936 as a daily service all the year round. This was an exceptionally popular holiday train usually composed of ten Pullman cars, though in the height of the summer these could be expanded to eleven or twelve. In addition to these named trains there were regular Pullman services to the other south coast resorts including Eastbourne, Worthing and Bognor.

The Devon Belle was the last Pullman express to be introduced in 1947, the last year of the Southern Railway. Though this train was shown in the timetables as non-stop from Waterloo to Sidmouth Junction, it stopped to change engines at Wilton and was not noted for its speed. It was really significant for the numbers of people it carried to the south-west. At its most popular it was known to consist of as many as fourteen Pullman coaches demanding a pulling power of nearly 550 tons from the engine. The job, however, was performed by the Bulleid Pacifics without too much difficulty. Another interesting feature of the Devon Belle was the observation car at the tail of the train. These cars had large windows on three sides and comfortable chairs arranged diagonally down the coach

The Brighton Belle gets its famous title. The scene at Victoria Station in June 1934 when the Southern Belle was renamed.

to provide panoramic views of the English countryside as the train raced on its way.

To service these prestige trains the Southern was well provided with impressive stations. In Waterloo, the company could boast the largest and one of the finest termini in Britain. Waterloo arose from the amalgamation of a collection of separate units, completed by the London and South Western Railway in 1922. By then the station comprised twenty-one platforms, linked by an impressive, broad concourse which curves around the ends of all these lines. It is flanked by the office buildings which came to be the Southern's headquarters. The office buildings were then fronted by the famous victory arch, commemorating the company's dead from the first world war. Besides increasing the number of platforms, the length of many of them had to be extended to accommodate bigger trains. No. 11 platform is 860 feet in length and 12, 13 and 14 are around 830 feet. Victoria is the other important Southern terminus. It originally consisted of two stations side by side: those of the London, Brighton and South Coast Railway and the London, Chatham and Dover Railway. When the two were united there were then seventeen platforms; later another six were added.

Last, but by no means least, came the Southern's steam locomotives. Building on the accumulated experience of Drummond and Maunsell, O. V. S. Bulleid was probably the Southern's most accomplished chief mechanical engineer. He served his apprenticeship with the LNER under Sir Nigel Gresley, designer of the famous *Flying Scotsman* and *Mallard* Pacifics. After being Gresley's personal assistant for fourteen years, he accepted Sir Herbert Walker's invitation to join the Southern and was then offered an almost free hand in the field of locomotive design. The first engine which he wholly designed was the Merchant Navy Pacific 4–6–2 class, completed in 1941. Its features differed markedly from any other English loco to date. Innovations included the all-

The Bournemouth Belle, headed by one of Bulleid's Merchant Navy Pacifics, hauls its train of Pullman coaches en route to the coast.

welded steel firebox, the valve motion enclosed in an oil bath and chain-operated, and disc driving wheels with indentations and holes for lightness. In appearance the engine was novel; the whole was enclosed in a thin steel casing to give a slightly streamlined appearance, said to be 'air-smoothed'. These flat, smooth lines gave Bulleid's engines a sleek, clean appearance. Although some of these features produced maintenance problems his engines were a great success. They were quick engines, capable of taking expresses up to and beyond 100 mph. The crews appreciated their design. The cabs were fully covered for all-weather protection; to help the fireman Bulleid incorporated a foot pedal to open the firebox door when shovelling in coal with both hands fully occupied. One of their drawbacks in the post-war economy period, however, was fairly high coal consumption. In 1945 Bulleid produced a modified Pacific design, the West Country class, a lighter and less powerful variant, for work in the south-west and elsewhere. The Battle of Britain class was similar.

From 1956 onwards, all the Merchant Navy class locomotives and sixty of the 110 light Pacifics were rebuilt. Ordinary Walschaerts valvegear was fitted and the air-smoothed casings removed. Some drivers resented the change, arguing that this was no improvement at all.

Probably the most famous of the light Pacifics was No. 34051 *Winston Churchill*, which pulled Churchill's funeral train to Bladon from London. Bulleid's most imaginative, and some might say least successful, exploit was the revolutionary 0–6–6–0 Leader class tank engine. Designed in 1949, it looked more like a modern diesel than a steam engine, and had two six-wheel bogies driven by chains from two three-cylinder expansion engines. The unfortunate fireman occupied a separate centre compartment with no side windows. The project was abandoned after considerable expenditure and few fruitful results.

5 Great Expresses of Europe

NICE (CIMIEZ).

The Riviera Palace

**SUMMER ON THE FRENCH RIVIERA
BY THE BLUE TRAIN**

The elegance and style of such great trains as the Golden Arrow was matched in Europe by a variety of world-famous trains. Such expresses as the Blue Train, the *Rheingold* and the Orient Express have become legendary.

As in Britain, the spread of railways in Europe was extremely rapid. The French government drew up a scheme for railway development in 1833. The first German line was opened in 1835. Austria followed in 1838 and Spain a decade later. Within decades, a network of railways had transformed the map of Europe. But the age of the great trains was handicapped in Europe by political frontiers. It was the genius of the Belgian Georges Nagelmackers and the *Compagnie Internationale des Wagons-Lits* which transformed railway travel in Europe. Nagelmackers was determined to do for Europe what Pullman had done for America and introduce comfortable through coaches operating over differing railway systems. The fruits of his efforts were to transform travel in Europe. Perhaps his greatest creation which has lived on in legend is the Orient Express, but to concentrate on this train is to forget some of the world's greatest trains running in pre-1914 Europe. Of these expresses, none achieved greater praise than *Le Train Bleu* (so called because of its blue and gold livery), running from Calais through Paris to Nice. Launched shortly after the Orient Express, *Le Train Bleu* made its first journey to the French Riviera in December 1883. For its rich and wealthy clientele (and those who hoped to be rich after a trip to what was then the world's most fabulous pleasure area), Nagelmackers's new express reached new heights of luxury.

Le Train Bleu offered the first travelling cocktail bar as well as a Pergola restaurant. The corridors of each ornate coach were carpeted in deep pile. Only ten persons were carried in each coach, under the ever-helpful charge of a servant-valet of *La Compagnie Internationale. Le Train Bleu* not only marked a new height in elegance in railway travel – it played a major economic and social role in the development of the Côte d'Azur into Europe's most famous playground, where the high society of a now vanished Europe met for the sole purpose of pleasure. The palatial hotels of Cimiez, above Nice, and La Turbie above Monaco were as much the creatures of this new age of railway travel as the Bahamas or Costa Brava have been of package holidays and air travel.

For English passengers, having begun the journey at Victoria (and no doubt fortified themselves on oysters or sole at Overton's restaurant for the journey to Dover and the three-hour cross-channel journey), *Le Train Bleu* was joined at Calais. The next stop, after a hectic dash through the French countryside, was Paris. At Paris *Le Train Bleu* became a truly international express. Carriages from elsewhere in Europe – from the Berlin of Kaiser Wilhelm, from the St Petersburg of a Russia where the Tsar still reigned supreme,

Previous pages:
The elegance and luxury of the *Compagnie Internationale des Wagons-Lits'* service to the Riviera as seen in the wealth of publicity material produced by the company.
Left:
Above The Riviera Palace, Nice, one of the many luxury hotels built by Georges Nagelmackers to accommodate passengers on his *trains de luxe.*
Below Dining in style in the restaurant car.
Right:
Above Uniforms worn by the company's staff in the period before the First World War.
Right One of the many striking posters produced to advertise the Blue Train.
Below The Blue Train at the Riviera in the 1920s.

and from the romantic Vienna of the Hapsburgs – met up to go forward with their human cargoes of princes and aristocrats to the Riviera playground.

Shortly after boarding at Paris, it was time for dinner in the Pergola restaurant while the train headed swiftly south through the lovely countryside of central France. Over the soup, fish, meat, cheese and dessert, news and gossip would be exchanged as the passengers planned their winter season on the Riviera. *Le Train Bleu* reached Marseilles and the azure Mediterranean coast the next morning. This was nearly journey's end. After Marseilles, the express wound its way more slowly along the coast, passing through frequent tunnels to reach Cannes, Antibes, and finally Nice. The winter season on the Riviera lasted from as early as the beginning of October to the following February, a season occupied with dinner parties and charity balls, promenades and shopping. It was a way of life which for many was to end when, with the assassination of the Archduke Franz Ferdinand in 1914, Europe was to be plunged into a war which destroyed her old empires. All this, however, lay in a mercifully hidden future. Even the war did not destroy the Riviera. A new world was called in to redress the balance of the old. Between the wars it became the turn of the Americans to transform the French Riviera as their summer resort. The Riviera survived, and with it the Blue Train. It is no longer so cosmopolitan, but it is still the principal overnight train from Paris to the south of France.

Although the age of Nagelmackers's elegance has vanished, railway travel in Europe still offers a degree of comfort and luxury which would be difficult to surpass anywhere else in the world. The Trans-Europe Expresses (TEE) are rightly world-famous. The pride of Germany, and one of the finest trains in the world, is the *Rheingold* (a TEE train since 1965). The *Rheingold* is first-class only, with a TEE supplement also payable. But it is the first name in excellence and worth every extra expense – it is a new experience in travel. For the English traveller boarding the *Rheingold* early in the morning after the sea crossing to the Hook, the resplendent dining-car offers a welcoming sight. The car is streamlined and sound-proofed, with both double-glazing and air-conditioning. A suitably English breakfast of piping hot bacon and eggs is served by the German or Dutch dining-car staff (the train is usually staffed by Dutch personnel as far as the German frontier). From the Hook of Holland, the *Rheingold* heads for Rotterdam. After Rotterdam the *Rheingold* glides swiftly and silently through a very typical Dutch landscape – flat countryside, with rich dairy farming and the inevitable windmills and drainage ditches – to Arnhem. The coaches are almost noiseless – just the gentlest sound of the wheels on the rail joints and the slightest sigh as the automatically operated corridor doors open and close. The comfort of the luxurious, fully reclining armchairs lulls one into a forgetfulness of the extra cost of TEE transport. At Arnhem, the last stop before the

A cutaway drawing showing the day and night-time arrangements of a wagons-lits carriage of 1878.

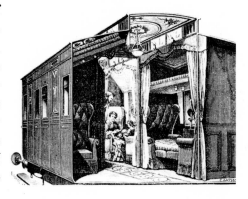

49

A Trans-European Express on the Paris-Brussels-Amsterdam service at the Gare du Nord, Paris.

German frontier, the engine crews change. The normal motive power in the early seventies, with steam only a memory in the past, changes to a German v200 class diesel. The v200 class, mechanically very similar to the British Warship class, are imposing engines which have established themselves almost everywhere in North Germany where electrification is not planned. At Arnhem, the *Rheingold* is joined by another portion of the express that has come from Amsterdam. The train then sets off on the next stage of its journey, through the relatively dreary frontier area towards Duisburg. Emmerich, on the frontier, is followed by the sprawling industrial conglomeration of the Ruhr. The *Rheingold* races through Wesel and Voerde before braking sharply for the various important junctions at Oberhausen, now in the heart of the built-up area, and so into Duisburg. Here further portions of the *Rheingold* (from Hanover) are connected and the express is ready for its race ever southwards down the beautiful Rhine valley to Switzerland.

In southern Europe the coming of the railways brought about a great transformation. Since the earliest days of history, the Alps have acted as a massive natural barrier between northern and southern Europe. In medieval times Alpine passes such as the St Gotthard were virtually the only routes between the two areas – and they were precarious, and passable only when the winter snows had melted. The railways completely changed this with the opening in 1882 of the St Gotthard tunnel. Originally the rail link between

50

Left The interior of one of the original carriages of the *Rheingold* Express. A high standard of comfort and service has been the hallmark of this service since its inauguration in 1928.

Below The *Rheingold*, now one of the great Trans-European Expresses, races through Oberwesel in the Rhine Valley en route to Switzerland.

The Simplon Tunnel, the longest railway tunnel in the world, links Switzerland and Italy. The two parallel bores beneath the Alps are seen here at Brigue at the Swiss end of the tunnel, which was electrified from its inception.

Zürich and Milan, 183 miles apart, took 7 hours. Now the journey has been reduced to a mere 4 hours. From very early days, this route was an obvious candidate for electrification. For fifty years, since the mid-1920s, electric traction has made this a showpiece line and an experience in rail travel. Despite competition – the Simplon route was opened in 1906 and the Lötschberg in 1913 – the St Gotthard route has continued to prosper.

Now a Trans-European Express, the *Gottardo* has always had the allure of one of the great trains of all time. Leaving Zürich *Hauptbahnhof* after breakfast, the electric *Gottardo*, now air-conditioned, sound-proofed and marvellously comfortable, gathers speed rapidly on the first stage of its journey to Arth-Goldau, the junction for the line to Lucerne. The *Gottardo* is now well on its way, passing through the pastoral countryside at the foot of the Rigi mountain. Next comes Schwyz, but despite the increasingly severe gradients the *Gottardo* still averages 70 mph through the seemingly endless series of tunnels along the wild shore of Lake Uri. The real

climb up to the Gotthard tunnel is now under way. From Flüelen, 1430 feet above sea level, with gradients increasing to one in forty, the *Gottardo* speeds on through Gurtnellen station, 2421 feet above sea level. Then comes the first spiral tunnel, a testimony to the achievements of the Swiss engineers of a century ago. Other spiral tunnels follow, until the famous landmark of Wassen church tower, 3044 feet above sea level, is sighted. Göschenen, 3628 feet up, marks the last station before the tunnel itself starts. For 16,502 yards the Gotthard tunnel carries the passengers and commerce of industrial Europe deep through the very heart of Europe. The journey through the tunnel itself takes a mere ten minutes – a savage contrast to the statistics surrounding the construction of the tunnel. The construction of the Gotthard employed over 2500 labourers, who toiled for seven years and five months at the cost of 177 lives before the boring parties finally met on 28 February 1880. Once the tunnel has been traversed, the *Gottardo* runs down to Lugano, Chiasso and Italy.

The Arlberg Express at Flirsch am Arlberg near the end of its long run from Paris to Innsbruck.

53

6 The Orient Express

On the evening of 5 June 1883 the Orient Express, destined to become one of the most famous European trains, left the *Gare de l'Est* in Paris for the first time. It was seen off by a large group of VIPs and an impressive band. Among those present was Georges Nagelmackers, the enterprising founder of the grandiosely named *Compagnie Internationale des Wagons-Lits*. This was the occasion of a considerable achievement, for he had succeeded in starting a luxurious through express service which overcame the rivalries of different railways and nations. Mortgaged to the hilt before it had even started, the Orient Express was the result of a devastating stroke of imagination, and was consequently a personal triumph for Nagelmackers. He had succeeded in operating a supra-national train running along track and pulled by locomotives belonging to others. His real genius was to have the vision to see what could be achieved with the existing European railway network, providing that the particular differences and unimaginative views of those who ran its various companies could be overcome. He created a single rail link between Paris in the west and Constantinople in the east.

Georges Nagelmackers had a remarkable early career. He was born in Liège in 1845 into a well-to-do family. His father was a banker and his mother of aristocratic family. As a young man he was handsome, and it was this quality which was in part responsible for his railway activities. For at the age of twenty-one he fell in love with an older woman who really only favoured him for temporary amusement. He took his rejection hard and emigrated to New York. At the same time that he arrived, the new Pullman Delmonico dining-car was unveiled, ushering in a new era of luxurious railway travel. Nagelmackers became a sightseer to distract himself from his jilted love. This American development was sufficient to inspire his financially gifted brain to consider the business of passenger travel. He returned to Europe at the end of 1868, with a germ of an idea. He then developed the idea of a company which would own the coaches to form through trains between several countries. The trains would run on existing railways and be hauled by the locomotives of those railways. Travel from one country to another was difficult then. Nagelmackers planned to offer superior accommodation and improved rail connections between European nations.

The Orient Express was the first of his international trains. Nagelmackers perceived his operations on a grand scale; it was to offer every facility and be finished with no expense spared. There was a smoking room, a ladies' boudoir and a library on top of the services offered by most express trains. The individual compartments or *coupés* were miniature drawing-rooms with appropriately Turkish carpets on the floors, inlaid tables and two red plush armchairs apiece. Since passengers had to sleep on the train as it

Opposite above A menu for dinner on the Orient Express on 6 December 1884, a year after the train was inaugurated.

Opposite below The elaborate interior of the restaurant car of the Orient Express, which was famed for its standard of service and *haute cuisine*.

The Orient Express in 1884 during the first year of its operation. It was the first of Georges Nagelmackers' great international trains and took 82 hours to make the journey from Paris to Constantinople.

raced across Europe, the silk-covered walls were designed to fold down to provide luxurious sleeping accommodation. Between each *coupé* was a mosaic-floored *cabinet de toilette*. Most spectacular at the time was the provision of shower cubicles with hot and cold running water. Most railways now provided restaurant cars, so Nagelmackers went to the extreme here. A special coach near the end contained the stores, including ice-boxes crammed with the most exotic of foods, and the servants' quarters. But the actual dining-carriage was the most lavish that Europe had seen. Its ceiling was covered with embossed leather from Spain; from its walls hung tapestries from the *Atelier des Gobelins*; and the curtains were of the finest Genoa velvet. A five-course dinner was provided, cooked entirely from fresh foods on board the train itself. After dinner, travellers retired to the smoking-room for port and cigars before going to bed.

Originally the Orient Express averaged a then-speedy 40 miles an hour, and called at the principal European cities – Paris, Strasbourg, Munich, Vienna, Budapest and Bucharest, and terminated at Giurgewo. There passengers crossed the Danube by ferry to join another train which took them to Varna, on the Black Sea, from where a steamer took them, eventually, to Constantinople. Nagelmackers took advantage of the variations in culture offered by the route. At Tsigany in Hungary, for instance, a gypsy orchestra came on board to entertain the passengers. From 1899 the train was able to run direct to Constantinople through Bulgaria.

Partly because of the wild eastern European terrain through which the train had to pass before reaching its Turkish destination, the Orient Express soon acquired an adventurous and romantic flavour. One story which was repeated on the run concerned a compartment occupied by two men and two women. One of the men was said to be a diminutive and silent Belgian. As the train entered one of its many tunnels the lights went out; there was a terrible scream. When the train emerged from the darkness into daylight the Belgian had disappeared. His body was discovered, so it was told, some miles back along the track, with the inside of his jacket lining ripped out. The three others in the compartment all testified that they had not laid a finger on him the whole time he had been in their presence, nor indeed had they even spoken to him. All they could recall of this mysterious event was the single piercing scream. Two government agents did in fact meet their deaths on the express, either being pushed or jumping from the train. It was also true that among Nagelmackers's worries was that political violence might break out on board among the cosmopolitan passengers. When, as sometimes happened during the winter, the train was trapped in a snowdrift in the Balkans, the *chef de brigade* immediately made his passengers swear on the Bible that they would not become involved in any political discussion, lest violence should break out. It was this atmosphere of danger and adventure which no doubt prompted writers like Graham Greene and Agatha Christie to use the express as a location for novels.

One of the train's most eccentric travellers was the deranged King Boris of Bulgaria. Originally his enthusiasm for railway rides led him simply to hire one of the train's private carriages – at some considerable expense. But he became bored with just sitting in a carriage. He sought permission to ride in the cab of the engine, and wore white overalls designed and made for him by his Paris tailor. But then he insisted on being allowed to drive the train himself. He was a reckless driver, taking no regard of signals or warning signs. Nagelmackers, fearing a serious accident, advised his officials to refuse him permission to ride in the cab. Undeterred, King Boris would travel in his special carriage until the train reached the border of his country. Here he would move down the train to the engine and defy the hapless driver to prevent him from driving the express across his own country. On one occasion when the king was driving at high speed there was a blowback and flames from the firebox set the fireman's clothing ablaze. Without a thought for his welfare the king raced the engine even faster, leaving the fireman blazing by the line where he had fallen. On arrival in Sofia, the besotted king offered himself to the passengers for applause for having got the train in on time despite the accident.

These episodes aside, the Orient Express had its own distinctive appearance. On the side of each carriage was the single, magical, compelling name 'Orient'. It conjured up an image of the near east: the 500 mosques in Constantinople, the Turkish atmosphere, the clamour of the casbah and the beggars in the streets. Once in the train the passengers relied upon the *chef du train*. Decked out in a blue uniform rather than brown, he was in charge of accommodation and seating in the restaurant cars. He was expected to be able to speak most European languages and was responsible for the safety of his illustrious travellers. To overcome all customs problems, as they passed through the various European empires, Nagelmackers issued his passengers with a special badge called a talisman. In the latter part of the nineteenth century, when the whole enterprise was conceived, cholera was still a threat in central and eastern Europe; consequently the timetables were styled 'cholera permitting'.

It was not only in luxurious fittings that the Orient Express scored over its rivals – its rolling stock was generally of superior quality, too. Nothing impressed foreign associates more than the result of a railway accident in Romania in 1889, between Bucharest and Jassy. In a collision the whole train broke up with the exception of one coach belonging to Nagelmackers's *Wagons-Lits* company. It was made of teak, which continued to be used because of its strength until the advent of the steel coach.

Lord Dalziel was a vice-president of the company. He was an astute financier and extremely ambitious man. He began his business career as a major ally of the American George Pullman,

A timetable for the Orient Express in 1909 covering the 2267 mile journey from London to Constantinople.

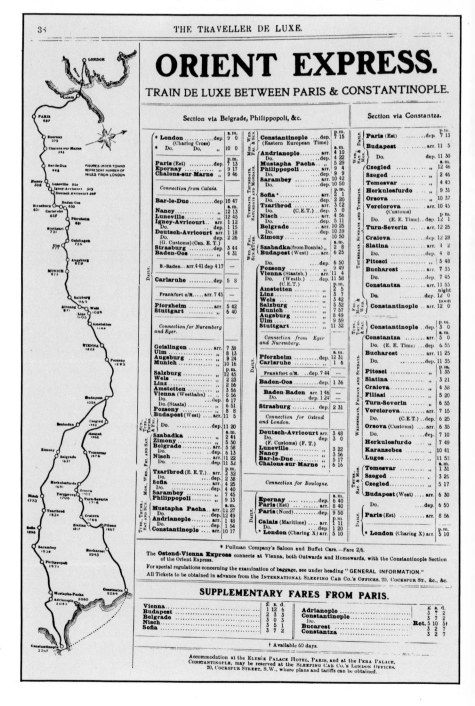

The risqué reputation which the Orient Express swiftly acquired inspired a bawdy Parisian musical comedy, advertised in this poster.

and, being a member of the English Pullman organization as well as the *Wagons-Lits* company he was able to propose and supervise a connection between the two. He developed a Pullman connection from London to Dover for Calais and then on to Paris and the Orient Express.

One Orient Express dining-car was to have a chequered career. The service was obviously disrupted by the first world war and the company retreated into Belgium to await the cessation of hostilities. Marshal Foch, the French commander-in-chief, had been making use of several coaches as his headquarters' office while the war was in progress. He decided that one of the luxurious dining-cars would make a suitable setting for the final signing of the armistice. He ordered car No. 2419 to be prepared for this occasion, and it was transported to Réthondes, near Compiègne. After triumphal appearances at the victory centres there was an unsuccessful attempt to instal the carriage at *Les Invalides*. It was eventually preserved in some gardens at Réthondes. This was not, of course, the end of its history. After the French had been defeated in the German offensive of 1940, Hitler insisted on having the car taken back to the same spot at Compiègne for the official signing,

Marshal Foch, accompanied by leaders of the British and French armed forces, posing on the steps of one of the coaches of the Orient Express after the signing of the armistice at Compiègne in 1918.

this time, of the French surrender. After this No. 2419 was towed back to Berlin. It was only destroyed, or so it appears, at the end of the war when an SS detachment was sent to blow it up in the town of Ohrdruf to prevent it falling into American hands. Again it had become a symbol of defeat.

Partly because of its air of adventure and mystery, the Orient Express is surrounded by a whole host of tales. On one occasion at an unidentified station in the Balkans the whole train was searched and passports were confiscated. One passenger was then ordered off the train by the military police and taken in great fear to the station-master's office. In fact, he need not have worried. It was the station-master's birthday and he had simply wanted to discover someone who was born on the same day so that he could share a drink with him. The express was held up for half an hour while these two drank champagne. Another story of embarrassment comes from *Reminiscences* by Colonel R. E. Crompton, a distinguished electrical engineer who had been responsible for the installation of electrical lighting at the Crystal Palace, and in many large European private houses. On one of his journeys to Vienna on the

Orient Express the following amusing incident took place.

I was sitting with my face to the engine in the outer seat of a table of four in the Pullman dining-car of the Orient Express. Another man was seated on my left and the two seat table to my right on the other side of the gangway was occupied by an Austrian lady and gentleman. On a curve just outside Munich, owing to a rail being out of place, our carriage suddenly leaned hard over to the left and I was forced violently against my companion. When the carriage righted itself I found that the Austrian couple had both fallen over, making a complete somersault. The lady's head had got underneath our table and her legs were upright in the air. While the other ladies screamed with laughter and the men endeavoured to keep grave faces, I grappled with the difficult task of holding the inverted lady's petticoats together and at the same time freeing her head from the table legs.

After I had succeeded in disentangling the lady, her husband thanked me and handed me his card. He was an Archduke. I handed him mine and thought the matter was at an end. But three days later I received a pressing invitation from the Archduchess, asking me to call at her house at the hour of afternoon coffee as she wished to thank me personally for the service I had done her. When I went into the room, the Archduchess got up from her chair and came forward telling her guests, chiefly ladies, 'This is my English friend, who saved my life and has seen more of me than my husband himself.'

The Orient Express in 1969 photographed entering Halkali, Istanbul where steam locomotives are exchanged for electric ones.

The Orient Express was considered sufficiently prestigious and important to be mentioned in the Versailles peace treaty. It contained a clause to the effect that the train should be started without delay, though defeated Germany pleaded, with a certain amount of justification, that the locomotives were worn out and the track was in a poor state.

To travel on the Orient Express was a very expensive business, as might be expected, but this was all part of its mystique. It cost about £58 per person or a total of £160 for a couple with a servant. The discounted £44 for a servant's fare was about their total annual wage. Yet it was this very concentration upon opulence and luxury which ensured the success of the whole enterprise. For the established aristocracy and the rising European *nouveau riche* made wealthy by industry and business flocked to travel on the Orient Express because of its very lavishness. It was a train with status; a train to boast about having travelled on. As Nagelmackers' enterprise grew in popularity and as his profits increased, so the train and its fittings and services became more luxurious. Bell-pushes were placed in the compartments, enabling travellers to summon maids from the servants' quarters. The servants employed by the railway company itself were kitted out in uniform and wigs which smacked of pre-revolutionary France. The food offered became more exotic and elaborate and a fully equipped bathroom was added to the amenities.

One further reason for the Orient Express's success was the contrast offered by Constantinople. The train's great comforts and services offered a sharp contrast with the primitive conditions of the Ottoman Empire. There was little for the unadventurous tourist who demanded high standards of cuisine and accommodation to do but simply get back on the express and return to western Europe. So Nagelmackers expanded his enterprises. He was responsible for building two of the most lavish hotels the world has ever known, both for the convenience of Orient Express passengers lost in a squalid country. The first, called the Pera Palace, he built in Constantinople. It featured marble-walled palatial rooms, a vast mirrored staircase and a spectacular glass lift encased in wrought-ironwork. The bedrooms, of vast proportions, were sited to overlook the Golden Horn. Nagelmackers's other majestic hotel, the Therapia Summer Palace, was situated on the shores of the Bosphorus across the straits from Constantinople. The whole lavish enterprise flourished, disrupted only in 1914–18, until the second world war.

7 The Trans-Siberian Railway

The building of the world's first transcontinental railway, linking the Atlantic and Pacific seaboards of North America, served as an inspiration to Russia. The construction of the Union Pacific and Central Pacific line was completed in 1869. As Britain was able to colonize and develop the African continent, so the Russians felt they could open up their eastern and central heartlands for considerable profit. It was thought that Siberia could develop into a useful new market and source of raw materials. It would also, it was believed, help to solve the problem of rural over-population in European Russia. This had produced dangerous famines in the past, resulting in riots and disturbances. The terrible famine of 1891 gave

Above A salon on the Trans-Siberian in 1900, complete with piano on the far wall. First-class passengers could enjoy considerable luxury, as Georges Nagelmackers was quick to adopt the line for one of his great international expresses.

Inset An advertisement for the Trans-Siberian Railway in 1898 when an attempt was made to sell tickets to Western travellers before the line was complete. In fact this particular excursion never took place, due to lack of would-be passengers.

Construction work on the section of line from Ekaterinburg to Chelyabinsk in the Ural Mountains in 1895. Women labourers can be seen in the foreground.

extra point to encouraging more peasant families to emigrate to the virgin but fertile lands of Siberia. But immigrants had so far been deterred by the long and hazardous journey involving a complicated combination of river boats, carts and railways. It has been estimated by some sources that one-tenth of adult and one-third of child emigrants died *en route*. But those intrepid travellers who had succeeded in getting as far as western Siberia had clearly demonstrated that this underpopulated land could produce cheap grain and some dairy products. There were, therefore, good economic and social reasons why the railway should be built. In addition, the statesmen amongst the Tsar's advisers were quick to see the purely strategic benefits resulting from the construction of a good communication link with the eastern half of Russia. A railhead would do much to spread Russian influence into Korea, Manchuria and China, and the naval and shipping bases of Vladivostok and Blagoveshchensk would be considerably promoted by a rail supply route.

But a project of such size and scope was not one to be easily undertaken. Though plans were first drawn up in the 1850s, work on the railway was not actually begun until the 1890s, and it was only in 1905 that a through rail link between Moscow and Vladivostok was complete. In the 1880s the Russian government began to think seriously of a Trans-Siberian Railway through from the west to the Pacific. But since most ministers, including the minister of ways and communications, considered that a Trans-Siberian Railway was not yet a practical proposition, it was basically Tsar Alexander III's enthusiasm which was responsible for its conception. He urged the construction of the Samara-Chelyabinsk line and the commencement of a line from Vladivostok. Indeed, his heir was selected to lay the foundation stone at Vladivostok in 1891. In the following year Witte, the minister of finance, revealed the plan for the railway. Since the migration of peasants from western Russia was one of the principal objects of the scheme, he proposed that this exodus should be planned so that land distribution schemes, as well as veterinary and religious facilities should accompany the construction of the railway line. Because of the immense scale of the enterprise he also proposed that the line should be built in clearly defined sections. His whole plan received royal approval in the end of 1892. The establishment of the Siberian Railway Committee marked a very real turning point, and its chairman, significantly, was Alexander's heir Nicholas. In a letter to his son Alexander enjoined Nicholas to carry out 'to the end this Russian project of peace and enlightenment in the East. May the Almighty help you to achieve this enterprise so close to my heart, together with the proposals to facilitate the peopling and industrial development of Siberia!'

One part of the whole plan was the construction of the Ussuri Railway, between the port of Vladivostok and the provincial capital of Khabarovsk. Typically the line had to be cut through a mixture of *taiga* and forest. But before the actual line could be built 400,000 roubles had to be spent on building roads in the area to supply the railway workers. The line from Ob to Irkutsk was a separate section called the Central Siberian Railway and possessed an individual character of its own. The hilly nature of the country provided the chief obstacle to the construction of the railway. Excavations and embankments were needed over most of this section. In the valleys of the Berezovka and the Sytik there were eighty-five bridges and culverts. In addition, the *taiga* was often covered by a thick layer of marshy ground which was frozen solid in the winter, often remaining like this until July. Here, as elsewhere, it was first necessary to build rough roads and then dig drainage ditches before removing the old layer of vegetation. Rails and metal fittings had to be brought great distances. The whole matter was complicated by lack of fodder for the supply horses. Labour was so short in this remote area that convicts had to be imported from the island of Sakhalin; they performed a function similar to the Chinese coolie in America or Australia.

Along the southern shore of Lake Baikal, high mountains stretch almost to the water's edge, and it was quickly realized that construction of the railway would be a difficult and protracted business. As a temporary measure, a train ferry service was started across the lake, using ice-breaking ferries ordered from England. This service was started in 1900, though it had to be temporarily closed down in the winter when the ice became too thick; horse-drawn sledges replaced the ferries. It took five years to complete the line around the tip of Lake Baikal, which was an exceptionally difficult piece of engineering. The lake was overhung by a line of cliffs which had to be penetrated by the Russian engineers. This feat was achieved only by boring thirty-three tunnels. The highest point of the Siberian Railway is here where it passes over the Yablonovy Mountains some 3400 feet above sea level. By 1904, the Trans-Siberian Railway was completed as far as Svetensk.

The construction of the final links in the Trans-Siberian Railway has an interesting history. In 1895 it was proposed to bridge the gap between the Trans-Baikal and Ussuri Railways by a route through Manchuria direct to Vladivostok. It was an attractive proposition because it had certain geographical advantages and would effectively serve to strengthen the Russian sphere of interest in the Far East. This then was the Chinese Eastern Railway. Because of her recent defeat by Japan, the Chinese government responded favourably to the Russian request for railway powers in Manchuria and in 1896 agreement was reached. It was decided that the CER would be a private undertaking financed by the Russo-China Bank. It was agreed that the CER Company would operate the line for eighty years, though after the first thirty-six the Chinese government had the right to purchase the line. Work was begun in 1897 but not finished till 1904 owing to the Boxer Rebellion. During this uprising Chinese government troops who were supposed to protect the railway joined the rebels attacking the European contingents and bombarded the railway. By the time the rebellion had been put down by a relief force, as much as two-thirds of the railway completed by 1900 had been destroyed. This was not the only reason, however, why the railway was not completed till 1904. The terrain was very mountainous. Eight tunnels had to be bored and two bridges of considerable size were built over the river Sungari. Its completion marked the end of a considerable engineering feat.

Having been soundly beaten by the Japanese in the Russo-Japanese war of 1905, the government decided that the CER was too vulnerable to attack and that they should complete the Trans-Siberian route on Russian territory by building the proposed Amur Railway, to link up the Trans-Baikal and Ussuri Railways. There was a lot of opposition from within Russia by taxpayers who felt that its value in no way measured up to its cost, for it was planned to run through largely barren and unpopulated land. Support for its construction came mainly from the inner cabinet of Russian ministers who saw its strategic implications. Stolypin, the prime

An early photograph of the Trans-Siberian showing a train crossing the Utka River bridge.

Left The station at Tsvetkovo, 1896, typical of Siberian railway stations.

minister, was a particularly ardent advocate. The railway was designed to run fairly close to the Manchurian border and for this reason proved to be a particular expensive undertaking; engineering considerations were undoubtedly being sacrificed to political and military interests. Problems were also created because the valley floors were prone to flooding, which meant that a raised embankment had to be built for the track. The railway was finally permanently opened to traffic in 1916. It had been one of the most expensive Russian railways to complete in terms of cost per mile.

The actual value of the construction of the Trans-Siberian Railway cannot be measured by its passenger receipts. For the line was never a paying proposition. It was through the achievement of its wider aims that the railway may be said to have been a success. Immigration increased to such an extent that the population of the area served by the railway increased by almost two million between

1900 and 1909. This is not, however, an accurate measure of total immigration as many people did not stop in Siberia but were tempted to continue on to the Far East. In 1902 alone over one million passengers were carried.

Because the Tsar was anxious to get the line built as quickly as possible, technical specifications were deliberately kept low. This decision was also influenced by lack of capital. The majority of bridges were built of wood rather than the more permanent but expensive steel used elsewhere. Those that were properly built were the big ones which were worth constructing soundly right from the start. Apart from these savings, there were other economies which proved to be costly in the long run. There were too few crossing loops and watering points, and the permanent way was not sufficiently ballasted, so that the track itself tended to creep on the gravel bed. Economies in materials were also dangerous. The rails tended to be too light and lacking in strength. The bridges, being made of light materials and on poor foundations, developed twists and gaps due to the continual thawing and freezing of the subsoil in which they were planted. Engineers had also built lines running up steep gradients to save making cuttings. These tended to slow trains down to a crawl. Hence, when it was realized that there was an ever-growing backlog of freight, these were some of the first sections of line to be improved. It was also decided that a double-track line would greatly speed up travel. By 1918 this project had been completed. The Russians were then able to claim that the section between Omsk and Kitaiskii (2262 miles) was the longest double-track stretch of railway in the world. In fact, this was slightly inaccurate as the bridges remained single-track.

Originally, travel on the Trans-Siberian railway was not a particularly pleasant experience. When Lenin was exiled to Siberia in 1897 he wrote that the farther one travelled the slower the journey became. There was initially an acute shortage of rolling stock for immigrants; in 1908 funds were laid aside to build fourth-class vehicles for Siberian immigrants. The first-class carriages soon gained a reputation for luxury comparable to those in Europe. At first the Trans-Siberian express ran twice weekly, with the state railway providing the engines and the International Sleeping Car Company the carriages and dining-cars. In 1903 it was decided to provide a *de luxe* train once a week with additional restaurant facilities. One of the best descriptions of the service at the turn of the century is provided by the American traveller Shoemaker. He made his journey in the winter of 1901–2 when the Irkutsk trains were starting from Moscow. He failed to get a passage on board one of the 'International' luxury trains simply because the official would not tell him when it ran. He had, therefore, to make do with one of the standard Russian trains financed by the government. According to his account it consisted of four carriages which were electrically lit; two of these were second-class, one first-class, and the fourth was a composite vehicle containing dining-room, kitchen and luggage compartment. In comparison to the rather shoddy facilities provided by the state service the 'International' train featured private toilets, writing tables, fitted fashionable carpets and bathrooms appointed with marble tiles and porcelain baths. On the even less expensive ordinary trains, Shoemaker reported that the third class was full but the first and second were empty; but the poorest of all, the immigrants, had to travel in *teplushki* which were humble freight cars fitted with bunks.

The reason why the railway failed to make a profit on its passenger traffic was not lack of travellers but simply that the government felt it was worth subsidizing immigrant passengers. It provided special incentive fares to attract people to the east, and so worked the railway at a loss. The government, in fact, attempted to make good this loss by trying to attract more first and second-class passengers, hoping to pull travellers away from the shipping companies that plied between Europe and the Far East. In 1903 special return tickets were issued which permitted the passenger to travel in one direction by sea and so enjoy the comforts of both types of travel. Another arrangement concluded with this end in mind was with the Canadian Pacific, for round-the-world bookings via Vladivostok, Japan, Canada and Liverpool.

Both the first world war and the civil war which followed resulted in severe disruption to traffic on the Trans-Siberian. Because of the general disruption caused by the war, marshalling yards away from the front became crowded with miscellaneous vehicles. Another source of difficulty was the German advance into the Ukraine before the signing of the peace at Brest-Litovsk, which cut off supplies of Donetz coal and created an evacuation problem. However, by early 1918 fuel stocks had been replenished. Railway workers suffering from the effects of food shortages often left their posts to search for sustenance. It was only the efforts of the railway executive committees which prevented serious stoppages and arrested potential strike leaders. The railway system, however, remained in a chaotic state until the 1920s and the introduction of Lenin's New Economic Policy.

The Soviet Union has continued to regard railways as a vital means of transport – at any rate for freight: the railway timetable has been known to commence with an exhortation to intending passengers to go by air and leave the railways clear for goods! Railways have been extensively modernized, not least the Trans-Siberian, much of which has been electrified. Curiously the name Trans-Siberian Express seems never to have been bestowed officially: quite possibly it was originally given by English travellers. Certainly the long-distance trains over the route now are called Russia, Baikal and Yenisei. Only the Russia traverses the whole route from Moscow to Vladivostok, and takes eight days to cover the 5811 miles.

8
Union Pacific

The vast continent of America offered a massive opportunity for railway pioneers. It was an opportunity eagerly seized. The railways, as much as any other single force, opened up the interior of the country. Thus the lands to the west of the Appalachian fold mountains were only exploited and populated after the construction of the railroads. They were of great significance in this continent's history and development. The history of America and the history of its railways are inseparable.

There were a few horse tramways built in the early part of the nineteenth century; for example the Delaware and Hudson Canal Company's line running in Honesdale, Pennsylvania, was built in 1829. Work started on the construction of the Baltimore and Ohio Railroad in 1828. It was North America's first long-distance line, intended to link the Atlantic seaboard with the Mississippi valley.

The company at first intended to use horses, but on completion of a substantial section of track-laying, it arranged for a locomotive contest on similar lines to the Rainhill trials held for the Stockton and Darlington Railway in Britain and won by Stephenson's *Rocket*. The company had been able to offer steam traction before this competition, but with little success. A local Baltimore resident, Peter Cooper, a gluemaker from New York and amateur inventor, had produced an experimental loco called *Tom Thumb* which had made the occasional trip along the line. It was, however, technically limited and was rejected in favour of a competition. There were five entries, all American. The winner was Phineas Davis, a watch-maker, who entered the engine *York*, a four-wheeled machine with a vertical boiler. It was a practical proposition and a further eighteen engines were built and continued to be used by the company until 1893. However, it proved impossible to enlarge the design, and eventually it died out. The president of America's first steam passenger railway was the plump and pleasant Philip E. Thomas (1776–1861), a merchant banker. Once he saw the success of the scheme, he ordered its expansion. By the time of his retirement in 1836 he had extended the line to Harper's Ferry and built a further 36-mile branch to Washington. By this time its success was clear for all to see. It had gross revenues of over 260,000 dollars per annum, seven locomotives, over 1000 freight cars and forty-four passenger coaches. Its next president, Louis McLane (1786–1857), a former cabinet member in the Jackson administration, pushed the Baltimore and Ohio on to Cumberland in 1842, though further westward extension was slowed partly by the high mountains and partly by opposition from the states of Virginia and Pennsylvania who feared competition. It was not until Christmas Eve 1852 that the last spike was driven in, when the line actually reached the Ohio river at Wheeling, Virginia.

These early developments in the railway era in America have been much overshadowed by one of the greatest projects in the

Opposite The scene at Promontory Point, Utah on 10 May 1869 when the locomotives of the Central Pacific (left) and the Union Pacific (right) steamed slowly towards each other and the construction of the first trans-continental line was complete.

71

history of railways anywhere in the world: the building of the first railway link across the continent. On the morning of Monday 10 May 1869 the teams of labourers and engineers working from either side of the American continent met near Promontory Point to complete its construction. It was the climax of many years' arduous and testing work, and the celebrations were on a fitting scale. The two companies, the Central Pacific working from the west and the Union Pacific from the east, agreed that the last 20 miles separating them should be laid 14 to 6 respectively. The arrangements for the 'ceremony of the Closing of the Gap' were elaborate indeed. Whole delegations of interested shareholders and dignitaries who had been involved in this massive enterprise were brought to Promontory Point by special trains. In addition there were unofficial excursion trains from either end of the 1725-mile line, and travellers from well beyond the termini of Sacramento and Omaha. State governors and important government officials were represented. The sidings laid down in the area of Promontory Point were crammed with excursion trains and individual passenger cars, which ousted the hard-worked flat-cars which had been used to convey the workers. To commemorate the completion a special mahogany sleeper bearing a silver plaque inscribed with the names of the chief officials of the Central Pacific Railroad was laid down. It also bore the legend, 'The Last Tie Laid on the Completion of the Pacific Railroad May 1869'. The spikes used to secure the track to this sleeper were also of no common stamp. Two of them were gold, the third a gift from Arizona fittingly cast in a mixture of gold and silver, and the fourth, which was donated by the state of Nevada, was solid silver. A vast crowd was assembled to see the two engines approach one another and halt, and watch the final spike hammered home. The newly established telegraph line was now connected and the famous signal sent, 'Done', at 12.47 eastern time. The swelling chorus of cheers broke into a storm of applause echoed by the shrieks from the locomotives' whistles. The two engines moved slowly forward and made contact, symbolizing the link between east and west in the American continent. The job was done.

The construction and projection of this railway has a long and interesting history. Throughout the late 1850s and early sixties various projects were put forward, but little came from these early efforts. What was needed was someone with vision and authority to lay down the law. Such a man turned out to be President Abraham Lincoln, who was largely responsible for the undertaking's inception. He considered the scheme carefully, and made it his duty to extract information from a whole variety of sources. One of those he consulted was General Grenville Dodge, who had built up a breadth of experience campaigning in the mid-western territories against marauding Indian tribes. He was an interesting choice as he was to become engineer-in-chief of the Union Pacific. The sum of Lincoln's researches was the famous Act of 1862, passed when the

civil war had been raging for a year without end in sight. The Act
was designed to 'aid the construction of a railroad and telegraph-
line from the Missouri River to the Pacific Coast and to secure to the
Government the use of the same for postal, military and other
purposes'. Evidence of Lincoln's involvement in the scheme is also
provided by the Act's stipulation that 'the track upon the entire
length of the railroad shall be of uniform width, to be determined by
the President of the United States'. These early plans all exhibit one
feature in common, optimism. This was to be a critical factor in the
completion of this enterprise. For the difficulties the engineers were
to encounter, the hazards, hardships and dangers they were to
experience were to surpass their most pessimistic of expectations.
What they were about to undertake proved to be one of the most
remarkable engineering feats accomplished in the nineteenth
century. General Sherman, Dodge's former commanding officer,
was to describe the feat as a 'work of giants'.

The construction started on opposite sides of the continent at
points some 1800 miles apart. The Central Pacific Railroad
contracted to work eastwards from Sacramento to meet the Union
Pacific Railroad working west from Omaha. The Central Pacific
was the first to begin. In January 1863 Governor Leland Stanford
of California, also president of the company, made a short
speech in Sacramento. He followed this by digging a small hole at
the place destined to become the western terminus of the
transcontinental railway. Then the engineer of the western team,

Top Locomotive and workers at Salt
Lake Valley in 1868 during the
construction of one of the many trestle
bridges on the Union Pacific line.

Above Workmen drill a hole in which to
set a charge of blasting powder during
the boring of a tunnel beneath the
Wasatch Mountains, Utah.

A 'Pony' locomotive, used for the transport of men and materials, photographed during the actual construction of the line.

Charlie Crocker, made a speech. He called for not three but nine cheers to set the project off, ending his speech with the words, 'Now then, the talk is through, and labour commences!' Crocker's enthusiasm and spirit were enormous, and, most important, were conveyed with infection. He inspired everybody with whom he came into contact. The thousands of work-hardened labourers, mostly Chinese or Irish, whom he employed, were nicknamed 'Crocker's Pets'. It is curious that Crocker was neither a trained engineer nor even contractor. He had been the owner of a prosperous dry-goods store. When asked what qualification this gave him to build a railway Crocker would justify his appointment with the argument, 'None, but I know how to handle men.' This was indeed no idle boast. He started work at a lightning pace. A regular fleet of schooners was soon sailing into Sacramento with cargoes of enormous redwood piles, 30 feet and more in length. These were to be the supports for the bridge over the American River. Other boats carried the important consignments of iron rails to build the 60 miles of track to the bridge. So skilfully did Crocker manage the sub-contractors working for him that within six months of the inaugural ceremony the river bridge had been built, and 18 miles of route had been graded and awaited the laying of track on its surface. The bridge was a considerable engineering feat. Consisting of two spans of about 200 feet in length, it was suspended 6 feet above the highest recorded water level. Not long after, Crocker took delivery of his first locomotive, called, after the president of the company, *Governor Leland Stanford*. It was a splendid sight, guaranteed to excite popular imagination. The boiler was painted blue-grey and bound with polished brass strip; the driver's cab was maroon outside and light green inside, and bore the loco's name in gold lettering on either side. The large driving wheels were painted scarlet, the chassis bright green and the steps to the cab orange. The loco also sported a large brass bell. Chimneystack and cow-catcher were also scarlet, while the tender was maroon picked out with orange lining, surrounding the initials of the company, CPRR, in gold – a dazzling sight.

The first really important obstacle which Crocker was to encounter was the Sierra Nevada mountains. The terrain became increasingly difficult for the engineers as they climbed into the rocky ranges. No straight lengths of track were possible as the slopes became ever more steep. To combat this, the line was forced to swing round on long sweeping curves carried over a succession of steep ravines on trestle bridges which demanded hundreds of thousands of feet of heavy timber transported from the port of Sacramento. In an attempt to save costs Crocker's engineers tried to fill in some of the smaller ravines with earth and stone from the areas through which they had passed; but the soil cover was so thin and the underlying rock so thick that they were unable to dig up sufficient rubble to build the embankments. Waiting for the massive supplies of timber was one of the frustrations facing Crocker. The bridges were impressive structures when completed. One of them, spanning Deep Gulch, was 500 feet in length and 100 feet high at its centre. Another obstacle to speedy construction was shortage of labour. There were not enough local workers, and Crocker was forced to hire Chinese for assistance. He began his recruiting in San Francisco where there was a large Chinese quarter. Later, when he had exhausted this reserve, he hired men through agents in Canton. The Chinese workers were a great success. Crocker wrote of their abilities, 'They are proving nearly equal to white men in the amount of labour they perform and they are far more reliable. There is no danger of strikes among them.' They were not immediately popular with the existing work force which was often of Irish origin. The Chinese workers usually organized themselves into groups of about a dozen or so, with a head man whose job it was to negotiate with the contractors and to keep order within their ranks. They also demanded their own food: they were accustomed to eating seaweed, bamboo shoots and cuttlefish, and also demanded vast quantities of rice and pork to be cooked in peanut oil and washed down with strong tea sweetened with molasses. Dressed in their baggy pantaloons, curious basket hats and sporting long black pigtails,

A poster issued by Union Pacific in March 1867, when 300 miles of the line westwards from Omaha had been opened to traffic.

they must have looked a curious sight alongside the Irish and American workers toiling on the slopes of the Nevadas. The labour force was to swell to a massive 10,000 on this stretch of the line. The hostility which had originally been felt between these groups of workers was soon dispelled in the companionship of gruelling labour, to be replaced by a mutual trust and guarded affection.

The enterprise closely resembled a military campaign. With every few miles completed a new base camp was erected consisting of supplies, medical facilities, a telegraph station and machine shops. Work was temporarily halted in November 1866 when winter fell on the builders, now at Cisco some 6000 feet above their starting point. They were within 15 miles of the Sierras' twin summit ranges. But this winter was to be one of the severest on record; it was nine months before they were able to continue with their work. Then the blasting and digging began all over again to cut a path through the tough granite which faced them. Faced with the problem of keeping his large army of workers employed during the winter months, Crocker set them to building tunnels where they would be untroubled by the heavy snowfalls and blinding blizzards.

These tunnels presented tough engineering problems. The granite was so hard that it made drill heads break without making any substantial impression. The solution was to hack out a bore and then fill this with explosive to blast a path through. However, even this method often failed to work, and the plug would shoot back out like a missile when the explosive was detonated, leaving the granite unscathed. Casualties were heavy while such experimentation was going on. Progress was painfully slow; a fast rate was as little as one foot in twenty-four hours' continuous working. The tunnels varied considerably in length. The longest, known as the Summit tunnel, was nearly a third of a mile, some 1660 feet. Because of the low temperatures and the snowfalls the Chinese workers engaged on the project tended to live underground while construction was in progress. Anxious to do the best he possibly could, Crocker sent to England for expert tunnellers; in response to his offer Cornish miners travelled to America to take part in the working. However, these men with their fine reputation proved inadequate for the task, and were always outmatched by the Chinese tunnellers. The Cornishmen eventually left in a rage of humiliation declaring that they were not accustomed to working on sites with yellow men and it was this that was putting them off.

The blizzards of February and March were the worst of all. Some workers were buried alive in their shacks as a result of massive falls of snow. The snow would build up around the walls of the huts until they were almost enveloped. In one instance a huge snowfall pushed a hut off the slopes and down into a ravine while its occupants were unaware of what was happening. It was then precipitated into a snowdrift some 60 feet deep where the trapped men were slowly suffocated to death. There were also cases of isolated groups of

The Union Pacific in the 1870s. Sunday morning in the day saloon.

workers killed by localized avalanches as they toiled along the line of the railway with supplies. But the summer came at last and the tunnels were completed. The gaps between the tunnels were levelled out and prepared for sleepers and rails. Reno was passed and the worst of the mountains was defeated. It was a matter now of moving out along the plains to meet the men from Omaha.

In the east, the Union Pacific had been slower off the mark; but having got started it set off at a cracking rate. Its task here was much easier than in the west, since it had an almost level terrain to aid its progress between Nebraska and Cheyenne. While the Central Pacific was fortunate to possess a man of Crocker's talents, the Union Pacific was lucky to secure the services of General Grenville Dodge. Dodge, like Crocker, was not initially an engineer; he was a soldier who had learnt engineering in the course of his surveying and fighting. He was to be assisted by another General, Jack Casement, and his brother Dan, who were to prove champion track-layers for the Union Pacific. One disadvantage they had, in contrast to the west, was the lack of a supply port. Omaha was a small inland town with no special facilities. Materials had to be stockpiled before any work could be undertaken. Apart from the problems of extended supply lines, marauding Indian tribes roamed the country. These were the fierce Sioux and Cheyennes, angered by the thought of the white man penetrating their home and hunting lands with the 'iron horse'. These tribes were continuously on the warpath throughout the three years that the Union Pacific was cutting across the central areas of America, and provided a constant irritant to the workers. The advance parties of surveyors, like the actual workers themselves, always had to be protected by armed guards of soldiers and by Pawnee scouts, traditional enemies of the Cheyennes. Workers always kept loaded carbines close at hand in case of Indian cavalry attack. Most of the workers, however, had been involved in the civil war and were able therefore to handle their guns skilfully in action.

By the end of their first year these men had succeeded in constructing 200 miles of line and this was to be stepped up in the following year, 1866, when 260 miles were completed. Their most difficult problems were still to come with the Black Hills, the deserts beyond and then the Wasatch range. The workers in these sections were accommodated in large box-cars consisting of three tiers of bunks, kitchen, canteen and superintendent's office. Every inch of space in these cars was used; the roofs, for example, were used to store the rifles and carbines. In the summer the cars became unbearably hot and stuffy; often, workers would prefer to sleep in the open under canvas rather than endure the atmosphere of the bunks.

Having reached the Black Hills, Dodge made the claim that his men would construct a further 500 miles of track in the following year, 1868. With this in mind he boosted his labour force, mostly Irish, up to the 10,000 mark and started in earnest. They were now working in true desert lands, and passed over the Black Hills with the aid of numerous trestle bridges. Because of the vast quantities of goods and equipment required to build the railway small towns in its path expanded and new towns were created by the business which it brought. One of the more notorious was Julesburg, nicknamed the 'Wickedest City in America'. It attracted every type of crooked hanger-on determined to get his hands on the earnings of the railway workers. There were gambling halls, drinking saloons and gangs of thugs who would not hesitate to steal if these more legitimate methods failed to produce cash. The only way to tame the town once this situation had developed was to declare martial law. General Dodge ordered his deputy, General Casement, to take in a force of men and restore order to the township. The town disintegrated once the undesirable businesses were forced to close down, as it was based on very little else. After five months of vivid life it became a ghost town. However, settlements of this kind continued to spring up and then die, as the railway crossed the continent. Catering for the needs of the rougher elements among the workers, they came to be known as 'Roaring Towns'.

The desert lands were a fearsome obstacle. The railroad had to pass over some 300 miles of the Red Desert before it came to Salt Lake City. Water had to be transported as the builders moved forward, adding to their supply problems. The extremes of temperature were crippling. The heat was unbearable during the day, but dropped sharply at night, so that men might suffer from sunstroke in the afternoon while others died of exposure in the evening. Again the snow and cold of winter stopped them short for months; they had now reached Wasatch. Ogden, a township a few miles to the west, had been agreed as the meeting place for the teams of workers from east and west. It was not to be a definite stopping place, however, and the team which got there first was to continue past that point until it met the other. There was now, therefore, an element of challenge in the building. There was also an economic

Passengers on an observation car pass the shores of the Great Salt Lake.

incentive to win the race, for the more line a company was able to build the greater was its ability to charge for freight and passengers, as this was done on a per-mile basis. Competition between the two companies was rife. There were contests to see who could lay the greatest distance of track in a day. The Union Pacific was able to push its daily rate of two miles to nearly three, and then to four. At one stage the Central Pacific, in response to this challenge, managed to lay 5½ miles a day for a fairly continuous period. Casement was furious when 6 miles were claimed. He reorganized his gangs, selecting the best men for this work. 'No damned Chinks,' he declared. They managed to achieve a magnificent 7½ miles; but Casement was not satisfied: he wanted 8 miles a day. Crocker replied with the boast that he would lay 10 miles. Casement believed this to be a task beyond the strength of his Chinese workers and bet him 10,000 dollars that it could not be done.

Eventually a pitched battle between the western Chinese workers and the Irish from the east could not be avoided. As the two lines approached each other the Irish began jeering. They could provoke no response from their rivals. Even well-aimed stones and clods of earth had no effect. Taking up their pickaxes and hammers the Irish charged the Chinese. Enraged by this assault, the Chinese fought back fiercely and gave the Irish a thrashing, making them flee back to their own lines. Having been defeated in a fair fight the Irish responded by making small bombs from explosives and lobbing them into the Chinese workers. The Casement brothers were called in to see that their workers behaved. But before the animosity finally ended the Chinese responded with one huge detonation, causing a massive landslide, killing and injuring scores of Irish gangers. The horrific nature of the incident stunned the two parties into truce. On 3 March 1869 the railway was completed as far as Ogden. The Union Pacific had succeeded in building some 1000 miles of line. Promontory Point was now being cited as the meeting point of the two companies. Their directors got together and agreed that they should publicly declare this place to be their junction; the place where rivalries would end. It was with the completion of this final section that Charlie Crocker achieved his boast of 10 miles of line constructed in a day. He did this very cleverly. For by regulating his daily schedules he was able to achieve his own 10 miles in a day and then leave his rivals a shorter stretch of line to build so that they were unable to respond to his challenge. By lunchtime on 28 April 1869 his men had completed 6 miles. By sundown they had laid one-third of a mile over the stipulated limit. There were now less than 10 miles of open ground in between Crocker's railhead and the Union Pacific workers. Crocker had won. Shortly afterwards the line was completed and the transcontinental railway from Sacramento in the west and Omaha in the east had been completed against incredible odds.

Opposite The Union Pacific today: a characteristic diesel freight train in the Weber Canyon, Utah.

9 The Great American Railroads

The building of the Union Pacific symbolized the aggressive, boundless spirit of the railway age in America. This spirit was to be seen in other railroads, such as the Southern Pacific and the Denver and Rio Grande.

The Southern Pacific was in the forefront of the great American railroads, and the section which crosses the Sierra Nevada mountain range in the west is the most outstanding. It has more curves and also traverses more mountainous territory than any other American railroad. The section of line under consideration here is that from Sacramento in California to Reno in Nevada. It is, of course, all part of the first transcontinental railroad completed in 1869, the Southern Pacific having absorbed the Central Pacific.

The railroad makes use of the Donner Pass, some 7000 feet high. In the eastward ascent the line was not laid upon the more obvious American River canyon, but was put down between the American and Bear rivers and above the West Yuba. Its course provides the traveller with tremendous views of chasms falling many thousands of feet, vast evergreen forests and polished granite peaks. These were all features stressed in early advertising campaigns.

In the winter the railway, running at these altitudes, experienced considerable difficulties. With the exception of Alaska, this area has the heaviest snowfalls in the whole of the United States. Blizzards and ice both presented tough obstacles not only to the builders but also to the operators of the railway once completed. Throughout the nineteenth century the comings and goings and the hazards of the lines were regularly reported in local newspapers. The railway was a lifeline for those situated either side of the Sierras; events were reported as occurring before or after 'the coming of the railroads'.

The gradient was incredibly steep, as much as one in forty-four for 18 miles. In addition, the whole 84 miles over the Sierras averaged out at one in sixty-four. Westbound, the gradients were easier and were steep for a shorter distance, only 13 miles. Constant improvement over the years changed the general picture of things. Now, with modern diesels and improved track, it is no longer a one-sided struggle against nature. By the 1870s the Southern Pacific had forty-two freight locos of a 4–6–0 type, supplemented by a large number of smaller 4–4–0s. Originally the line was constructed with a single track. To prevent it from being blocked by blizzards expensive wooden snowsheds were constructed, many miles in total length. During the summer, when the wood had dried out, these sheds, traversed by coal-burning steam engines, constituted a serious fire hazard. This was combatted by special fire trains, mountain-top observers and elaborate sprinkler systems, and by telescoping sections of sheds mounted on rails of their own. Innovation, good engineering and constant improvement made for progress on the Southern Pacific. It was eventually decided, under the influence of increased traffic flows, to make the track double all the way over the mountains. Work began in 1906. The final section to Summit Station was opened in 1925 after nineteen years of arduous work. As well as doubling the line the company laid steel rails to replace the weaker iron ones. This work was completed within the first eight years, and permitted heavier loads and larger and more powerful locomotives.

As with most of America's main trunk routes, the Denver and Rio Grande Railway was not actually constructed by the company itself but through an intermediary construction firm. These companies existed to make money solely through the building of railways and not from their actual operation. In this case the company was the

Workmen adding fill at Fort Madison, Iowa, in 1887 during the early stages of the building of the Santa Fe Railroad.

Above Fierce weather conditions were a recurring problem on the railroads. A picturesque early print showing sectionmen clearing the track for a snowbound train in New England.

Opposite above The Silverton branch of the Denver and Rio Grande Western Railroad passing through spectacular Rocky Mountain scenery as it approaches the canyon of the Rio di los Animas Perdidas – the River of the Lost Souls.

Opposite below A poster issued in the early 1870s by the New York Central and Hudson Valley Railroad advertising their four track lines, enabling passenger and freight trains to be operated independently.

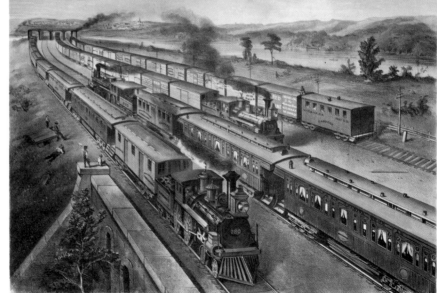

Union Contract Company, established in 1870 by charter in the state of Pennsylvania. Its principal officers included Charles Hinchman, an associate of General Palmer, and W. S. Jackson, a prominent figure in railroad circles. The arrangement worked as follows. The initial surveys for the route were made under the direction of the railway company itself but were actually paid for by the construction company, which was then to make its profits from building the line. The railway company was the boss; it selected the final route and laid down the specifications for the type of lines. The contract company then took over the building; it also equipped the line and initially operated it until the railway company demanded that it should take over. It was also required to submit periodical engineering reports to the president of the railway company. The construction company surprisingly was also required to negotiate for and to purchase all lands over which the line was to pass, though the deeds were made out to its employers; the money was refunded when payment was due. The first part of the building of the Denver and Rio Grande Railway is slightly confused. It was planned to construct it from Denver, Colorado, southwards almost into New Mexico at El Moro, having passed through the towns of Colorado Springs and Pueblo. For economy, the narrow gauge of three feet was adopted. The Union Contract Company started work on 1 January 1871 from Plum Creek, Denver. Work did not keep pace with schedules, however, and Colorado Springs was not reached by the gangs in July 1871, but only on 26 October. Delays were mainly caused by difficulties in obtaining the track, which had to be imported from Britain and Belgium. By August the gangs had got construction work up to the rate of $1\frac{1}{4}$ miles per day. The completion of this section to Colorado Springs also marked the opening of the railway for passenger traffic. There was a special opening ceremony when the loco *Montezuma* steamed the length of the track with local dignitaries and officials from the two companies involved. Operation of the line remained, nevertheless, in the hands of the Union Contract Company until 1 January 1872, when it was formally handed over to the railway for operational purposes.

The next section to be completed was from Colorado Springs to Pueblo. It was planned to complete this section within six months, finishing on 1 July 1872. This speedy plan was feasible only because a great deal of preparation had been completed; for much of its course the line had been graded and piled. Most of the building materials were also well on the way. There was some doubt as to whether the railway would actually go to Pueblo, but so keen were its inhabitants to have the use of the railway facilities that the railway company decided that it was a practical proposition to build a line to their township. This section was completed in April 1872.

The section between Pueblo and El Moro now came in for serious consideration. In April 1873 General Palmer, an officer in the railroad company, urged shareholders to undertake the completion of this route. Delay, he argued, could only stifle the economic development of the area and slow down the rate at which the company increased its profits. The line was actually laid as far as Cucharas by February 1876. Great efforts were made by General Palmer and his fellow directors to secure sufficient cash to fund the last stretch to El Moro, which was eventually completed on 20 April 1876. A regular freight and passenger service was established a week later.

From this point southwards, however, further progress was blocked by the Santa Fe RR which was being built south-westwards into the area the D & R G had hoped to serve. Instead, the D & R G built lines westwards among the Rocky Mountains to tap the rich metal-mining areas there. The terrain was very rugged indeed, and all the engineering skills of the period were needed to lay out and build these lines. There were loops, spirals, steep gradients, choking tunnels, all among spectacular scenery. These lines were built to the 3-ft gauge. Most were eventually widened or closed, but one narrow-gauge section is still operated for tourists, with steam engines, by the Rio Grande Company. This is the Silverton Branch, which is described in Chapter 13.

Railroads built America, but it was only steady progress in locomotive design that enabled them to do so. The years up to and including the 1860s produced the classic American nineteenth-century steam locomotive, the 4–4–0 with cow-catcher, headlight and balloon stack. It was a simple, functional and pleasant design, and the engines cost around 8000–10,000 dollars each. They often burned wood rather than coal, and were economical to run at well under a dollar a mile. This type of locomotive was steadily improved and made faster and more powerful. The climax came on 9 May 1893. Engineer Charlie Hogan, driving 4–4–0 No. 999 on the New York Central Railroad's crack Empire State Express, was said to have achieved a speed of $112\frac{1}{2}$ mph. It was the first time that a man-made vehicle had been recorded travelling at over 100 mph. No. 999 was specifically designed to haul light, fast trains. By the 1890s much larger and more powerful locomotives were already in service. The Baltimore and Ohio introduced ten-wheelers or 4–6–0s as early as 1863. By 1865 many lines were using Mogul or 2–6–0 locomotives. These had eighty-five per cent of the engine weight on the driving wheels, which was advantageous for hauling heavy trains. After several smaller lines were consolidated into the Lehigh Valley RR, a new and more powerful engine was designed. This was the 2–8–0: the wheel arrangement was called Consolidation in honour of the amalgamated company. The type became the standard American freight engine for the next quarter of a century.

By 1882 the Central Pacific was using vast (for the period) 4–8–0 locomotives for the climb over the Sierra Nevada, and even built an experimental 4–10–0 named *El Gobernador*. By 1900 the

Opposite above One of the colourful Southern Pacific locomotives, which hauled the famous Daylight expresses between San Francisco and Los Angeles, photographed at San Francisco in 1952 before the change to diesel working.

Opposite below Union Pacific No. 8444 on a special tourist run at Wyoming. This preserved locomotive represents one of the final designs of American steam locomotive power.

Above The eastbound Empire State Express at Dunkirk, New York, early in 1952, headed by an impressive New York Central Hudson locomotive.

A Union Pacific Big Boy, the greatest of the American Mallet locomotives, hauls a long line of freight cars through Echo Canyon, Utah in 1959.

4–6–0s generally used for passenger trains had been enlarged to weigh as much as 50 tons, while their goods counterparts, the Consolidations and Decapods (2–10–0s), weighed anything up to 75 tons.

The twentieth century saw the development of the Pacific type, the 4–6–2. Among the most famous of Pacific classes was the Pennsylvania Railroad's K4 class, which was first built in 1914 and then developed as the mainstay of the railroad's passenger motive power for the next twenty-five years or so. The Pennsylvania and the New York Central competed for New York-to-Chicago traffic, but whereas the PRR's route took it through the mountains, and meant that locomotives had to be designed for steep gradients, the NYC had its longer but easier 'water level route' through the valleys of the Hudson and Mohawk rivers and could build locomotives (like

999) for speed. In the 1930s it was using handsome, fast Hudson 4–6–4s introduced in 1927. But in 1947 these were superseded by what turned out to be examples of the last and finest generation of American steam locomotives, when the NYC introduced its great S–1 class 4–8–4 Niagaras. These locomotives weighed 210 tons, had a working steam pressure of 275 psi, and were fitted with mechanical stokers. They could equally well haul hundred-car freight trains or race from Chicago to New York with the twenty-car Twentieth Century Limited express, running for part of the journey at a sustained 85 mph.

Meanwhile freight locomotives had been growing larger too. The big step forward had come with the adoption of the Mallet type: this originated in Europe and its characteristic was that the locomotives had two sets of wheels, the front set of which could swivel; this enabled the locomotives to traverse sharp curves. The Mallet type combined a short fixed wheelbase with plenty of driving wheels. The early European Mallets were quite small, but the first built in the USA, a 0–6–6–0 placed in service with the B & O in 1904, was for a short time the largest locomotive in the world, and American Mallets rapidly grew bigger still. By 1913 the Erie RR had a triplex Mallet, a 2–8–8–8–2. Mallets of early design were unstable at speed, but later designs were refined so that they could be used for passenger as well as for freight trains. A remarkable example was the cab-first 4–8–8–2 type used by the Southern Pacific over the Sierra Nevada. The object was to move the engine crew to the front of the locomotive, where the view ahead was good and they were ahead of the smoke through tunnels and snowsheds. It was achieved by reversing the usual arrangement of parts of a locomotive, putting cab and firebox at the front and smokebox and chimney at the back: this was practicable because oil fuel was used and was piped the length of the locomotive from tender to firebox. The greatest Mallets, however, were Union Pacific's Big Boys. UP had come a long way from its pioneer days when in 1941 it introduced this class of 4–8–8–4s. Each of them weighed 350 tons and, up the grades from Cheyenne to Laramie, could haul trains weighing no less than 6000 tons. (In Britain, even today, 1000 tons is considered a big load!) The Big Boys remained in service until 1959 and several are preserved.

Among the greatest of expresses in the USA in the steam era were the Daylights of Southern Pacific. One of SP's most important routes lay along the west coast – from Los Angeles north to San Francisco (450 miles) and on northwards to Portland (another 712 miles). In the early 1930s the company saw stiff competition coming from other forms of transport and took action: in 1937 it introduced the San Francisco Daylight which ran from Los Angeles to San Francisco by day in 8½ hours, and the Shasta Daylight over the route from San Francisco to Portland. These were billed as 'the most beautiful trains in the world', and successfully counteracted

91

road and early airway competition. The locomotives, 4–8–4s, were the most powerful passenger engines of their day; they were semi-streamlined and painted in a striking livery of red, black and orange to match the trains. Whether they were really beautiful is a matter of taste, but as the ultimate expression of brash Americanism in locomotive design they were certainly superb, magnificent, fabulous. They hauled the Daylight expresses for seventeen years until diesels took over.

Much later, when the American bicentennial was approaching and a mobile, railborne exhibition was being created to celebrate it, one of these SP 4–8–4s was taken down from the pedestal upon which it had been preserved, motionless, since withdrawal. Overhauled, restored to working order and repainted in red, white and blue, it looked in 1976 as striking as ever as it hauled the American Freedom Train.

The two most important changes on American railroads since the second world war have been the replacement of steam power by diesel, and the near-extinction of the long-distance passenger train. With the American gift for doing things on a grand scale, the former was more complete, and quicker (in relation to its extent) than anywhere else, and the latter looked at one stage as if it might be total also. In the 1950s, airlines and automobiles drew passengers away from trains, and the railroads, prevented from quickly withdrawing uneconomic services by obsolete government regulations and labour union contracts, endeavoured to reduce their losses by economizing on the standards of service. This of course made train travel less popular still. By 1970 the number of long-distance passenger trains running had fallen by no less than ninety-eight per cent since the peak years of the 1920s. The trend was halted by the establishment that year of Amtrak, the government-sponsored National Railroad Passenger Corporation. Almost all long-distance inter-city passenger trains in the USA are now Amtrak trains which run over the systems of still-independent railroads. One of the few railroads which is an exception and still runs its own long-distance passenger trains is the Denver and Rio Grande Western. Otherwise, Amtrak provides locomotives, passenger cars, servicing personnel and marketing; individual railroads continue to own tracks, marshalling yards, signalling systems and stations, and to employ train crews. Despite initial problems and public scepticism, Amtrak has enabled great trains to continue to run in the USA, and has certainly made one noteworthy improvement, the establishment of a through service from coast to coast – sleeping cars are conveyed – from New York to Kansas City by the National Limited and on to San Francisco by the Southwest Limited. Not so long ago, critics of rail were all too willing to point out that whereas a pig could travel coast-to-coast in the same vehicle, mere human passengers were forced to change trains at Chicago!

10 Canadian Pacific

While few railways in Canada have ever been easy to build, the Canadian Pacific linking Vancouver on the Pacific seaboard with Ottawa in the east was perhaps the most testing and exacting from an engineering angle. Its construction involved the conquest of the northern part of the Rocky Mountains. The Canadian Pacific Railway has a long and distinguished history. It began in 1857 when an imperial commission was established by the British government, 'to inquire into the suitability of the Colony of Canada for settlement and the advisability of constructing a trans-continental line of railway through British territory from the Atlantic to the Pacific Ocean and

The driving of the last spike at Craigellachie in the Selkirk Mountains in November 1885 by Donald Smith, later Lord Strathcona. Behind him, in ulster overcoat and top hat is William van Horne, chief engineer of the Canadian Pacific.

thus connect at the same time to provide safer and more direct means of communicating with the British possessions in the Orient' – or so ran the official report. A British party then spent four years in the wilderness attempting to find a suitable route. Their leader, Captain Palliser, was pessimistic and recommended that the scheme be rejected. Consequently work was dropped until 1871 when the admittance of British Columbia into the confederation of Canada forced the government to agree to construct a railway from the Pacific Ocean over the Rockies to connect this western province with the Atlantic by way of the Great Lakes.

The work of exploration and surveying was entrusted to Sandford Fleming. His choice is not without interest; for besides being a famous engineer, he was also Chancellor of Queen's University, Ontario. He was presented with a formidable task. He was faced with discovering and surveying a route through the forests of Ontario, across the buffalo-tracked prairies of the Middle-West Territories and then over 500 miles of towering mountains before descending to the Pacific coastlands. From Ottawa to Red River, in Manitoba, they had to pass through largely unexplored forests. Their work in the prairies was much less arduous. It was in the Rockies that things became really difficult. Besides the mountainous nature of the terrain, they had to cope with rock falls, fallen trees, glacial torrents and a shortage of food caused by an unanticipated absence of game. Sandford Fleming and his team were engaged in this business for ten years. In 1881 the Canadian Pacific Railway Company was formed and events began to move apace. A fresh, southerly route through the Bow River and Kicking Horse passes was selected.

Once the route had been selected and surveyed, there came the mammoth task of constructing the line. Two phases of the great achievement stand out: the construction of the line along the shores of Lake Superior and the building through the mountains west of the Prairies. William Van Horne was appointed engineer-in-chief. In his preliminary survey of the lands surrounding Lake Superior he discovered what he later described as 'two hundred miles of engineering impossibilities'. The terrain was a mixture of rocky forest and swamp lands. Extensive engineering works were needed. Pessimists suggested that it would take twenty years at least to complete this section. In fact it was done in four. The cost, however, was enormous; twelve million dollars were spent, of which two million went in the purchase of explosives alone. Twelve thousand men of many nationalities, 2000 teams of horses and twelve steamers for the transport of material and provisions were employed in the workings.

Yet even this task is dimmed by comparison with the work undertaken in the Rocky Mountains. Jagged peaks, plunging canyons and powerful mountain torrents were their obstacles. The answer was to build tunnels, ledges and bridges of awesome aspect.

Opposite The Canadian, the transcontinental express from Montreal to Vancouver, running through the Bow River valley, Alberta with the Rocky Mountains in the background.

A vivid representation of the interior of an immigrant train on the Canadian Pacific in 1888.

Among the rank and file of the construction gang was a young man nicknamed 'Texas' because of the wide-brimmed hat he wore. When the job was done, this young man, Morley Roberts, wrote down his experiences in these railroad camps. His accounts vividly recall the atmosphere of the diggings:

In the daytime there was the usual labour, such as drilling holes in the rock to blast it with powder, whose explosion sometimes threw the heavy stones a hundred yards into the torrents of the foaming river. We would dodge behind trees and all get into sheltered places till the shot was fired, then come out again and take away the debris, hammering the larger blocks into pieces and shovelling up the smaller into carts. . . . Our camp was right on the banks of the river, which ran in a sharp curve round the base of the hill through which the tunnel was being cut. . . . Beyond this the hill ran up gradually into a maze of fallen timber, with one little melancholy cleared space, where a simple and rude grave held the body of an unknown and friendless man who had been killed some short time before I came. And still further on was the summit of the low hill under which the tunnel was to be.

The grave served as a nasty reminder. For, as Morley noted,

the work was of a hazardous and dangerous character. The hill was being attacked on both sides at once, and at the west end . . . the tunnel was advanced at some distance, but at the east end, though there too, the hole had been run into the hill, the work was to do over again owing to the tunnel having 'caved' in, in spite of the huge timbers.

When they were cutting into the hill to start the tunnel again, Texas reported that he never 'felt safe, for every minute or so would come the cry: "Look out below!" or "Stand from under!" and a heavy stone or rock would come thundering down the slope amongst us.'

While Canadians and Europeans worked from the west, 7000 men, mostly Chinese, were hewing their way from the Pacific seaboard eastwards. So inhospitable was the terrain that in a total of nineteen miles, thirteen miles of tunnel had to be constructed. In many places the track bed had to be hewn out of solid rock to form a ledge in the rock face. This work was of a particularly dangerous nature: the men were lowered hundreds of feet down an almost perpendicular cliff to blast a foothold on the mountainside.

By contrast the work on the prairies proceeded with a rapidity unparalleled in the history of railway construction. In a mere fifteen months, in which there was one interruption caused by the winter, 700 miles of track were laid. The whole set-up resembled a military camp. There were row upon row of sleeping tents with kitchens and stores besides. The builders devised their own commands. Dawn brought the cry of 'Roll out teamsters' from the 'corral boss'. The men rose and breakfasted; this was followed by the cry 'hook up' from the foreman, and the whole force would commence its first five-hour stretch of work. 'Unhook' came at noon and lunch was served, followed by another five hours' work before dinner.

The last gap in the route was closed when the construction teams met at Craigellachie. It was a spectacular spot situated in the Eagle Pass over which towered the mountains of the mighty Gold Range. On 7 November 1885 a special train was run up the line to the meeting place. From its passenger car, called Saskatchewan, stepped Donald Alexander Smith, a major shareholder in the company, William Van Horne, the engineer, and Sandford Fleming, the original surveyor. Donald Smith, who had been as responsible as anyone for raising the final injection of cash required to finish the job, was given the honour of driving the last spike into position. Sandford Fleming described this historic scene:

The work was carried on in silence. Nothing was heard but the reverberations of the blows struck by him. It was no ordinary occasion; the scene was in every respect noteworthy from the groups which composed it,

An early photograph of a Canadian Pacific train crossing a bridge over the Nipigon River on the northern shores of Lake Superior.

A dramatic picture of a partially collapsed bridge at Hearst, Ontario, during the construction of the Grand Trunk Railway in 1911.

and the circumstances which had brought together so many human beings in this spot in the heart of the mountains. . . . Most of the engineers, with hundreds of workmen of all nationalities who had been engaged in the mountains were present. . . .

All present were more or less affected by a formality which was the crowning effort of years of labour, intermingled with doubts and fears and of oft-renewed energy to overcome what at times appeared unsurmountable obstacles. . . . Suddenly a cheer spontaneously burst forth, and it was no ordinary cheer. . . . Cheer after cheer followed, as if it was difficult to satisfy the spirit which had been aroused.

Several hours later a message was flashed across the Atlantic from Queen Victoria; it was to convey her congratulations to the people of Canada on the completion of the Canadian Pacific railway. A great deal of the credit for the completion of this epic scheme must go to William Van Horne. He was possessed of almost tireless energies; his capacity for work was prodigious. 'Sleep', he once claimed, 'is just a habit. A habit to be indulged in only when absolutely imperative.' He had the ability to stay awake for incredibly long periods, catching short rests here and there. He was a man of powerful resolve.

Because of the length of the journey and the steep gradients necessitated by the Rocky Mountains, the Canadian Pacific was particularly anxious to finance the development of powerful steam engines. The passenger trains were usually of a lengthy nature, often some fifteen coaches, which meant a payload of around 900 tons. Ever larger and more efficient types of locomotives succeeded one another, expanding from the 4–6–2 type to 4–8–2s and 4–6–4s. Special engines were designed to pull trains over the Rockies and these were of a 2–10–4 wheel arrangement. These monsters were introduced in 1929. They were also distinguished by their massive tenders. Supported by twelve wheels, they carried 12,000 gallons of water and 4100 gallons of fuel oil: yet even these powerful engines had to be double-headed to get their trains up the one in forty-five gradients between Revelstoke and Kicking Horse Pass. A fleet of thirty was maintained to keep the regular service operating. Since then the diesel has taken over.

The other outstanding Canadian railway built on a large scale was the Grand Trunk Railway. It was originally conceived as a competitor to the Canadian Pacific, running to the north of its rival from Prince Rupert in the west through the Rockies at the Yellowhead pass, on to Edmonton and Winnipeg, and then skirting the north of the Great Lakes to join the St Lawrence at Quebec. Originally the Grand Trunk Railway Company concentrated its efforts around the northern shores of the Great Lakes. Lack of capital had prevented them from undertaking any more grandiose schemes. But in the first few years of the twentieth century, plans to construct a line to the Pacific were revived. In 1903 a Bill was passed and heavy government subsidies were promised. On 11 September 1904 Sir William Laurier, the then prime minister, turned the first sod of the Grand Trunk, or more precisely its Lake Superior branch. The Grand Trunk selected an area called Tuck Inlet for its western terminus and renamed it Prince Rupert; it was not a particularly wise choice for a terminus since it was subject to fog and heavy rain, and had little available space for the development of harbour installations and industries in general. The company decided to follow established practice and build simultaneously from several bases: Winnipeg, Prince Rupert and Fort William. A major error of construction lay in building this line to an unreasonably high standard. The policy of most American railways had formerly been to push through as fast as possible. Once the line had been completed, and income was rolling in from services, it was reasonable to improve the quality of the track. But the Grand Trunk made the mistake of wasting too much money and time in the building stage and so increased their debts while delaying the time when they could start to recoup these losses. The company's progress was also retarded by an acute shortage of rails and workmen. The first section to be opened in 1908 was that between Edmonton and Winnipeg. Work on the western section was still under way in 1911, and it was estimated that it would require another year and a half to finish it. Work was hampered by the fact that Canadian steel companies were unable to fulfil their orders, and high import duties meant that it was not feasible to import rails from either Britain or America. Shortages of labour persisted. The company proposed to bring in Chinese workers who had been so successful when employed in the United States. Though the company undertook to return all these workers when the line was completed, the government refused to allow them into the country. The Grand Trunk experienced not only those difficulties associated with the terrain which the Canadian Pacific had endured, but was also hampered by administrative and supply problems. It was not until New Year's Day 1913 that the Grand Trunk was able to despatch its first train from Winnipeg to Port Colborne. And it was not until 7 April 1914 that the last spike was driven home and the Grand Trunk and all its branches were complete.

11 Crossing the Australian Continent

Although Australia is a vast continent and its towns and cities are often separated by waterless arid deserts, it is not just geography which poses a problem for the railway system of the continent. The bane of Australian railways – and a hangover from the middle years of the last century – is the multiplicity of gauges. No less than five different gauges were adopted by the various state railways, with the result that today's total track mileage of over 20,000 miles is far less useful to the continent as a whole than it would appear.

In general, Australian railway practice has followed that of England, although American influence was also to be important. Thus, track sleepers are fastened to the rails direct by spikes rather than in the British way of setting them in chairs. But Australia itself has been a powerful factor on the evolution of her railways; lack of water and vast distances have favoured the replacement of steam by diesel and the development of luxurious 'Great Trains' for long journeys.

The very first beginnings of the railway age in Australia came in 1854, when the first train in Australia made its inaugural journey between Melbourne Flinders St and Sandridge (now Port Melbourne). From this initial two-mile trip, the modern railway system of Victoria has grown (Victoria now boasts the greatest mileage of any of the states proportional to its size).

However, the area which was to see the most spectacular railway developments in the next decade or so was not Victoria but New South Wales, where a system developed around Sydney. Interest in railways was evident from the mid-1840s when deputations forced the governor, Sir George Gipps, to lay the matter before William Gladstone, the then secretary of state. Lieutenant Woore RN was

The Hawkesbury River Crossing just
north of Sydney on the main route to
Queensland, a photograph taken in 1945,
showing the new bridge nearing
completion, with the old bridge, now
demolished, behind it.

The longest straight stretch of railway track in the world. The Trans-Australian Railway crosses the arid wastes of the Nullarbor Plain for three hundred miles without a curve.

hired to survey a route from Sydney. His plans, presented to a public meeting in January 1848, resulted in the formation of the Sydney Railway Company under the chairmanship of Mr Charles Cowper. However, construction did not get under way until 3 July 1850, when the Hon. Mrs Keith Stewart, daughter of the governor of the state, turned the first sod of the line in Redfern, a district in Sydney. Unfortunately the large crowd which assembled was soaked by heavy rain. Further delays followed as a result of a lack of local labour, attracted away by the gold rushes in the west. To solve this problem the company had to hire 500 men from England. The gold rush was also responsible for producing an abnormal rate of inflation, forcing the company into serious financial difficulties. The colonial government, wanting to see the railway completed, was forced to intervene. Under its auspices the line from Sydney to Paramatta was completed on 3 September 1855.

Four locomotives had been ordered from Robert Stephenson's workshops in Newcastle-upon-Tyne and the English carriages were supplied by Wright and Sons in Birmingham. These were described as being built of teak and of the finest standard, 'richly fitted in a most modern and fashionable style'. The 13 miles of line had cost £565,000 to build. The opening journey, again completed in pouring rain, took 45 minutes.

An early notice concerning one of the stations is of interest. It refers to Haslem's Creek or Rookwood Mortuary Station No. 1, opened in 1864: 'Train Fares to Haslem's Creek, Corpse carried free of charge, Friends of corpse one shilling each. Note, in the case of paupers' funerals corpses and their friends are carried free.' The line was extended westwards as time passed. It reached the Blue Mountains in 1863, the first real geographical barrier to its progress. Back in 1856 a preliminary survey had been undertaken by sappers of the Royal Engineers under Captain Hawkins. They were not hopeful. Eventually these hills were conquered by the intrepid efforts of the company's engineer, George Cowdrey, who constructed the famous Lapstone Zig-Zag. It has a gradient of one in thirty-three and two bridges, one spanning the Nepean river (the Victoria Bridge) and the other called the Knapsack Viaduct. These remarkable feats were both designed by the chief engineer and famous Australian pioneer John Whitton. Those associated with this section of line told fearsome tales of loco drivers descending the steep zig-zag on wet and slippery nights before modern air brakes were fitted to trains. Engines were put into reverse gear to stop them running away and diving headlong into Knapsack Gully. The only serious accident occurred on 22 March 1886, when a tourist passenger train from Bathurst with nine carriages and a guards van over-ran the points and collided with the buffer stops. The engine and two carriages were derailed and several passengers were injured.

Stations on the line appear to have been located for one of two reasons. One was the proximity of old coaching inns, established stopping points. Wascoe station, for example, was named after John Outrim Wascoe, the landlord of the Pilgrim's Inn nearby. The Blue Mountains station was built close to the old inn of the same name. The other reason was the presence of an influential personage able to persuade the railway to cater for his own needs. The company opened Lucasville in 1874 for the convenience of the Hon. John Lucas. In the following year it built Eager's Platform for Sir Geoffrey Eager who lived close by.

In 1868 the line was extended further west to Mount Victoria at Katoomba. On the section from Valley Heights to Katoomba are 20 miles of the steepest railway in Australia, rising 2280 feet between these two stations. The gradient is one in thirty-three for most of the way. In 1869 the line was extended to Bowenfels, involving the construction of the famous Lithgow Zig-Zag designed by Whitton and built by Higgins. John Whitton, though he was to become one of Australia's most renowned engineers, was by birth an Englishman. He had gained his early experience of railway construction in Britain. He had formerly worked on the Oxford, Worcester and Wolverhampton Railway and had been involved on the Manchester, Sheffield and Lincolnshire lines.

Work at Lithgow was begun in 1866. The hilly terrain required large-scale blasting operations. Two blasts were fired, detonated by an electrical charge – the first time that this method had been used. In all a quarter of a million yards of earth were shifted to construct the inclined sections. It was an exceptionally difficult task and the surveyors had at certain points to be suspended by ropes to carry out their work. Again, once constructed, this section proved to be a difficult one to operate, with the danger of slipping in wet weather. Speeds were sensibly restricted to 10 mph coming down and 15 mph ascending. But with the increase of traffic based on the expansion of trade and business, this section became a bottleneck by the 1880s. In 1910 the Zig-Zag was replaced by a series of tunnels and cuttings, another immense engineering task. The Lapstone Zig-Zag also was replaced by a tunnel, constructed in 1892. However, it was not particularly well designed and was badly ventilated. Drivers complained, but nothing was done until there was an alarming incident in 1908. A goods train was being driven up the line through the tunnel with assistance from a pusher engine. Unfortunately the leading loco stalled. While waiting for it to move on the rear engine's crew were overcome by fumes and decided to reverse out into the fresh air. Having recovered their senses they decided to return, just as the driver of the leading train also decided to back out of the tunnel. The collision which resulted produced a blockage which lasted for two days.

Like most old lines, the Western Railway has its famous express services. The Blue Mountains Evening Express was nicknamed 'The Fish' in the 1860s. This was because Jock Heron, its regular driver, established a reputation for fast running and challenged the signals at Penrith every evening. People used to say, 'Here comes the big fish.' Consequently the train crew was christened Salmon and Pike. The name 'The Fish' stuck and has been adopted as the official name for the service, which is now worked by electric multiple unit trains with stainless steel coaches.

In 1845 a Mr A. W. Scott proposed the construction of a tramway to Singleton from Newcastle by way of Maitland at a cost of £350 per mile, but nothing concrete came of his proposals. In 1850 Dr Mitchell of Burwood secured an Act of Parliament to construct a tramline from Burwood to the waterfront. In 1853 the partially completed line was taken over by the Newcastle Coal and Copper Company, and then finished. On completion it was thrown open to the public and steam locomotives were introduced. Given this spur, £100,000 was raised by subscription to extend the line further into the Hunter valley from Maitland to Newcastle. Mr Wallace of the Sydney Railway Company was appointed engineer. A locomotive was ordered from Fairbairn and Co. of Manchester at a contract price of £2250, and work began. However, the Hunter Railway Company also found itself in difficulty over the depleted labour market resulting from the gold rushes. The colonial government was again forced to intervene and arranged for a supply of workmen from England; the first batch arrived in Newcastle on the *Ellenborough* in November 1854. On the previous day, the fourth, the first sod had been turned by the chairman, Mr Kemp. Because of financial troubles the government had to step in again in 1855. By the end of the following year the line was completed; it consisted of nine bridges, nine culverts and a timber viaduct built over the tidal flats around Newcastle. On 27 December 1856 a train was run to Maitland for the Christmas race meeting there, with about 500 passengers on board. This train can claim to be the first race special in New South Wales, and probably in the whole of Australia.

A regular timetable came into use in March 1857 with four trains

The giant Hamersley Iron Ore train, sometimes hauling as many as 200 trucks, runs between Mt Tom Price in the north of Western Australia and Dampier on the coast. Given the immense distances and remote conditions of the Australian continent, the railways play a vital role in the industrial and commercial life of the country.

per day. Fares were as follows: two shillings and threepence first-class and one shilling and sixpence second-class to Hexham (the half-way stop) and five and sixpence and two and ninepence respectively for the whole trip. The extension of the line in 1858 to West Maitland, a further two miles, was the occasion of great festivities, triumphal arches, bands, speeches, levées, free travel, illuminations and fireworks. Throughout the 1860s the line was pushed further and further northwards; by 1883 it had reached Armidale and by 1884 Glen Innes. The last section, to Tenterfield, was opened in 1886. This remained the terminus until a link was made with the Queensland system in 1888.

With the forging of this connection the first train to Queensland was run, called the Northern Mail. The contemporary timetable showed that the journey took a total travelling time of 36 hours 22 minutes. The train left Sydney at 4.53 pm on 16 January and passengers arrived in Brisbane at 6.15 on 18 January, having changed into a Queensland train on the narrow 3 ft-6 in gauge at Wallangara. In 1937 a crack appeared in No. 4 pier of the Hawkesbury river bridge, after fifty years of constant use. A departmental inspection showed that replacements would be necessary. Train speeds across the bridge were first reduced to 10 mph and later to 4 mph. Only one train was allowed on the bridge at a time. Plans were then prepared for a new bridge which was begun upstream from the old one. A new bridge 2764 ft long and consisting of eight spans was constructed, and opened on 1 July 1946 by the

Hon. W. J. McKell, then premier of New South Wales. Two of the trains running on this line provided express services each way from Sydney to Newcastle and northwards. In 1954 the permanent way between Hawkesbury and Newcastle was strengthened to allow fast working.

Also in New South Wales, peculiar engineering difficulties were encountered on the line between Sydney and the mining town of Illawara. The section from Waterfall to Scarborough was troublesome to maintain in wet weather, owing to the steep nature of the country and the many patches of soft or 'greasy' soil on rocky hillsides. A red cutting south of Otford has the unpleasant knack of squeezing out stones of various sizes which either break windows of passing trains or bury the track. Landslides at Stanwell Park have occasionally resulted in track closure. Another point of trouble was the narrow ledge between Coalcliffe tunnel and Scarborough old station, which, owing to the sloping rock under the ledge, has a bad record for landslides. The construction of earthworks for the line sliced through the clay bands protecting the rock carrying the ledge. At one time there was a very real danger that the whole of the village of Clifton might be pushed over the cliff into the sea below. The railway responded to this threat by constructing a series of brick galleries and culverts to carry off the water that falls down the hillside in periods of heavy rainfall and causes constant seepage. These culverts have continually to be kept clean, as sudden and heavy rain will bring about the renewed danger of landslide if this is not done.

Western Australia was another area which witnessed the growth of an important railway network. Although it was the first portion of the continent to be discovered, it was the last to be opened up for settlement. It was not until 1829 that English settlers arrived at Swan River and a proper colony was established. The first railways here were late even by Australian standards. The very first was built privately in 1871 to transport timber to Lockville from the Karri forests. Another was built at about the same time from Rockingham to Jarrahdale, but it too was solely an industrial railway. The government was the real moving body behind railway construction. It was responsible for the line between Geraldton and Northampton, some 33 miles, opened in 1879. Another line followed in 1881 from Fremantle to Perth and then Guildford.

But the real stimulus to railway building was yet to come, and that was the gold rushes of the 1890s. In 1887 deposits were discovered at Southern Cross, 240 miles east of Perth. Then more gold was found at Coolgardie in 1892 and again at Kalgoorlie in 1893, which all produced a demand for improved transportation. Lines were extended throughout the southern half of Western Australia. Heavy traffic from the goldfields necessitated smoother gradients over the Darling Range. On 1 July 1896 the main eastern line was diverted from its original route to run from Bellvue to

Mount Helena through the new Swan View tunnel, 370 yards long up a one in fifty-five gradient.

Not unnaturally, the last Australian lines to be built were those which crossed the great desert lands. Like the mountains, they presented difficulties of their own – lack of water, fever, the heat and distance from civilization. Originally there were plans to build two great desert railways; one to run north–south down the centre of the continent from Darwin to Adelaide, and the other to run east–west from Port Augusta to Kalgoorlie, effectively linking Melbourne to Perth. The first to be commenced was, however, never completed. In 1888 the first 70 miles of the Great Northern Railway were opened; it ran south from Darwin to the town of Adelaide River. The line eventually got as far as Mataranka. What was unusual was the use of Chinese coolie labour. This was the only Australian railway in which labour shortages necessitated the import of Singhalese and Chinese workers, and 3000 were used. But more important for future schemes was the use of camels for moving both men and materials to the work. In 1865 122 camels had been shipped with their keepers from Karachi in India to Port Augusta. The men in charge of the camel teams were invariably called Afghans or 'ghans', though only a few actually came from Afghanistan. Most of them had emigrated from Rajastan and Baluchistan (now West Pakistan). Even Persians, Egyptians and Turks were called ghans. Gathered together at Beltana they manned the greatest camel-breeding stud farm in Australia. It was owned by Sir Thomas Elder and Samuel Stukey. The Beltana Camel-Carting Company eventually spread through much of central Australia. Indeed, by the time the railways began to push north from Port Augusta in 1879, Beltana camels were famous. They were certainly used to construct the last big railway project in Australia, the Trans-Australian Railway, running from Port Augusta west to Kalgoorlie. Although various projects had been mooted, including the formation of a grand syndicate in 1881 headed by the Duke of Manchester and the Earl of Denbigh, the cost and nature of the terrain had prevented any practical achievements. But finally, after five years of hard toil, the 1051 miles of railway were opened in October 1917.

The Trans-Australian is the longest and indeed one of the greatest railways in Australia. From Kalgoorlie in Western Australia to Port Pirie in South Australia is a distance of 1,108 miles, across some of the driest and most inhospitable terrain anywhere in the world.

The statistics of the engineering feat which made this line possible are remarkable. The line has no tunnels and no bridges. In one of the toughest and most arduous construction epics in history, no less than 3,000 men (aided by steam shovels, horses and camels) carried out the laying of $2\frac{1}{2}$ million sleepers, 140,000 tons of rails and the shifting of a massive 5 million cubic yards of earth and rock. Water – especially in the Nullarbor plain – was virtually non-

Southern Aurora, the luxury overnight express between Sydney and Melbourne, Australia's two most densely populated cities.

existent. At very heavy cost, wells and bores had to be sunk to provide essential water for the original steam traction (now long since replaced by diesels). In an area where there were no streams for a thousand miles, even these bore holes proved disappointing. In many cases, the water was not fit for human consumption and rotted the boilers on the locomotives. Decent water had to be brought a distance of up to 500 miles. Not surprisingly, camels proved to be of great value in the desert and the laying of the Trans-Australian was the last time that these animals were put to use in Australia. The workmen on the line faced tremendous extremes of temperature – ranging from 120 degrees Fahrenheit in the shade during the blistering summer days, to below zero at night in winter.

Sixty years after the inauguration of the first section of the route (on 22 October 1917), a transformation in passenger styles and comfort has taken place. The Sydney–Perth journey (2461 miles) now takes three days. At first, the line closely follows the route of the early Australian pioneers – Blaxland, Lawson and Wentworth – who made the first crossing of the Blue Mountains way back in 1813. After traversing the Blue Mountains the Trans-Australia passes the famous mining centre of Broken Hill and then on via Port Pirie and Port Augusta to the Nullarbor limestone plain. Nullarbor itself means 'without any tree', a title that is fully justified.

In railway records, the Nullarbor Plain boasts the longest stretch of straight railway track anywhere in the world – no less than 297 miles without the hint of a single curve. In the air-conditioned comfort of the train, the passengers look out on the scant Nullarbor vegetation of bluebrush and saltbush. After conquering the Nullarbor, the Trans-Australia continues its journey via the goldfield city of Kalgoorlie and on to the sheep-farming country around Perth. It is a remarkable journey in a land that is still young.

110

In 1970 this special excursion train, piloted by a Pacific class locomotive, covered the Trans-Australian route from Sydney to Perth and back, powered entirely by steam.

Over the years, the motive power on the 'Trans', as it is affectionately known, has also seen great changes. Although steam locomotives were used at first, a host of factors made an early change to diesel traction a priority. Apart from the high cost of coal and water, the poor quality of the water took its toll of the engine boilers, whilst the sandy nature of the track also wreaked mechanical havoc. Hence, in 1951, a Clyde GM class diesel was introduced. Weighing 108 tons, its 1500 horse power quickly brought about substantial economies on the route. Partly, also, the diesels benefited from important improvements to the track. By 1945, nearly all of the route had been ballasted and 94 lb rails welded into 270-foot lengths had replaced the old track. The motive power on the 'Trans' now consists of two 3780 horse power Class 46 electric locomotives which haul the train from Sydney. Once over the Blue Mountains, the motive power is replaced by two 1800 horse power Class 44 diesel-electrics for the run across the flat plains of western New South Wales. At Broken Hill, another change of locomotives takes place, with a single 1800 horse power Class 600 diesel-electric of the South Australian Railways taking over. The next major change occurs at Port Pirie. Here the entire crew change as well as the locomotive. From Port Pirie, the 'Trans' is taken over by a single 3000 horse power Class CL diesel of Commonwealth Railways. For the next 1107 miles to Kalgoorlie, the class CL is in charge across the endless Nullarbor plain.

The final locomotive exchange occurs at Kalgoorlie. For the remaining 408 miles to Perth the engine is a 3300 horse power Class L unit of the Western Australian Railways.

The 'Trans', although overshadowing some other expresses by the very length of its journey, is far from being alone among the 'Great Trains' of Australia. In addition to such historic expresses as the

Blue Mountains express The Fish and the Indian Pacific on its Trans-Australian haul, there are a wide variety of other expresses worthy of note. Among them is the Silver City Comet. This began running between Parkes and Broken Hill (New South Wales) in 1951. It was the first complete train in Australia in which air-conditioning was used – the run of 422 miles is through particularly dry and dusty territory. Important changes occurred in New South Wales in the 1950s when a number of these new air-conditioned daylight expresses were introduced on routes previously served by night express or mail trains. These expresses, which brought about a revolution in train travel in New South Wales, included the Sydney–Melbourne Daylight, the Monaro, the Northern Tablelands, and the North Coast Daylight.

Of the contemporary expresses, particular mention must be made of the Southern Aurora. This express began in April 1962 with the completion of the new standard-gauge line between Albury and Melbourne. Its stainless steel sleeping-cars, all fully air-conditioned, include dining and lounge cars. The sitting passengers on this train are conveyed in a supplementary express, the Spirit of Progress. Another Australian express also serving Melbourne is The Overland. Over the years, this express which connects Adelaide and Melbourne has built up a well-deserved reputation for efficiency and comfort.

Since 1953 Queensland has also introduced some of the finest expresses in Australia, although speeds are not particularly high. Of these Queensland expresses, the most interesting is the Australind. Its non-stop run of 99 miles from Perth to Bunbury is the longest on the Queensland system.

Opposite above The Deniliquin Mail, headed by a Beyer-Peacock locomotive, photographed at Wagga Wagga, New South Wales in 1958 before the changeover to diesel traction.

Opposite below The Indian Pacific Express, eastbound from Perth to Sydney, photographed at Hesso, South Australia.

The Victoria Falls Bridge, part of Cecil
Rhodes' dream of a Cape to Cairo
Railway. A Beyer-Garratt engine hauls a
mixed train southwards from Zambia
into Rhodesia in the 1950s.

12 The Garratts of Africa

A hundred years ago even South Africa, now the most highly developed and economically advanced of the African countries, possessed a mere 55 miles of railway. It was constructed, significantly enough, to the standard British gauge of 4 ft $8\frac{1}{2}$ ins. With the discovery of diamonds near Kimberley in 1873 a powerful incentive was created for an efficient transport service to the mines from Cape Town. Six hundred and fifty miles of railway were then laid down to link the two. The line was completed in 1885 but for economy reasons the gauge was deliberately reduced to 3 ft-6 ins, which then became the standard gauge in South Africa.

It is impossible to look at the growth of the railway systems in Africa without looking at imperialism, the driving force which gave them life. European nations gradually explored and annexed the larger part of Africa between 1880 and 1900. To secure the riches of these lands and to establish hegemony over them, this conquest was usually linked with an economic plan which involved laying down railway networks. In British colonies these railway systems were usually funded from the mother country. The engineers and the track and rolling stock were also of British origin. Cecil Rhodes's vision of a railway running from the Cape in the south to Cairo in the north was not simply the dream of a businessman. He felt that such a line passing through this extended line of British possessions would place an imperial unity on them all. In the event, this line was never completed, but the suggestion serves to show how closely connected were the notions of empire and railway construction.

The British were in many ways most successful in colonizing South Africa and Rhodesia, and here their railways may be seen to best effect. After the burst of railway-building inspired by the opening up of South Africa's diamond mines, the country's growing

The opening of South Africa's first railway from Cape Town to Wellington in 1864. A contemporary engraving showing the arrival of the first train at Wellington Station.

population and wealth provided a further stimulus for construction. Lines were then built from Port Elizabeth, East London, Durban and Delagoa Bay to Johannesburg, and these comprised the backbone of the South African system. All these lines were constructed on the 3 ft-6 ins gauge. However, there were some anomalies. For example, in the northern part of South-West Africa there were about 350 miles of line laid down to a 2-ft gauge. These remained until the volume of traffic became so great as to make transhipment to the 3 ft-6 ins gauge at Usakos, on the Windhoek–Walvis Bay line, impracticable. In 1960 these lines were relaid with 3 ft-6 ins gauge track. This area also suffered from a further drawback in the days of steam. The rainfall was low with an average of only 6 inches in the south and 20 inches in the north. Droughts were also common and the very high temperatures meant that what little water there was tended to evaporate very quickly. Conditions were therefore not at all favourable for running steam locos; water was simply too scarce. So gauge conversion was not unnaturally accompanied by a switch to diesel power. However, it should not be thought that steam has disappeared from South Africa altogether; for there are good economic reasons why it should stay. The country still has an abundance of coal with a low production cost. As a result it has been South African policy to electrify all lines where traffic is heavy and gradients are steep since this power can be generated by coal. Diesels have been adopted on lines distant from the coalfields themselves and where there are water shortages, while steam engines have remained where coal is readily obtainable and water easily supplied.

Railway locomotives were initially supplied by Britain. In Rhodesia, on the Beira Railway for example, some of the earliest engines were purchased from the Falcon Works. These were largely 4–4–0 tender locos and were designed to run on light, narrow-gauge lines. In the light of later developments their tractive effort was

Preceding pages:
A fine view of the Port Elizabeth-Cape Town express hauled by a Beyer-Garratt locomotive, with characteristic tender in front and auxiliary water tank behind.

Above The first train from Umtali to Salisbury on the Beira Railway. The slogan on the front demonstrates how much the Cape to Cairo project had captured people's imagination.

Left An illustration from a French magazine of 1903 claiming to represent the building of the Cape to Cairo Railway.

Above On the Maclear to Sterkstroom line, Cape Province: a South African Railways 19D hauls the daily passenger train out of Maclear on one of the most dramatic steam-worked lines in the world.

Right A Garratt engine at Victoria Falls Station, Rhodesia heading a Zambia-bound freight train.

A 38 class Garratt hauls a goods train over a spectacular viaduct on the Kisumu line in Kenya. The Garratt engines were widely adopted by East African Railways.

puny indeed, a mere 3000 lb. The makers boasted that their engines could haul 158½ tons on the level and 24 tons up a gradient of one in forty. As time passed and the traffic on these lines increased, the designs were modified to increase the engines' power. When they ran on the Beira Railway the locos were neatly painted in black with yellow lining, though some of the later ones were given a green livery with yellow and darker linings. At about this time the Cape Government Railway and the Bechuanaland Railway Companies put in orders with the famous Glasgow engine builders, Neilson & Co. They were looking for more powerful locos for the proposed Cape-to-Cairo service. Neilsons and other Glaswegian builders continued to supply large numbers of locomotives to South Africa around the turn of the century, while a batch of a similar design were sent to the Sudan in 1897. No doubt this order was inspired by the idea that the two ends of this mighty continent could be linked by a single railway.

Two engines which were purchased about this time had an interesting history. They were bought to run on the Mashonaland Railway in 1899, numbered 5 and 6, and named *Inyanga* and *Paulington*. Originally built by J. Fowler and Co. of Leeds, they were first run on the Metropolitan and Suburban Railway, which had been laid between Cape Town and its suburb of Sea Point. These locos had not proved successful on this line, for being 0–6–0s they were unsuited to the sharp curves of the track and were frequently derailed. When this company was forced to close in 1897 the engines were first sold to the Cape Government Railway. They were then renamed *Sea Point* and *Green Point*. However two years later they were sold to the Mashonaland Company for just over £2000. Featuring brass-capped chimneys and domes they were, apparently, smart-looking tank engines; they ran well for their first few years in service, but suddenly deteriorated and had to be put on to shunting

A 60 class Garratt with a mixed train passes close to a Kenyan village.

duties at Salisbury and Umtali, where one was nicknamed *Pretty Polly*. Finally, they were sold to a private contractor in the 1920s when the loads at the yards became too heavy.

With the extension of the railway from Bulawayo to Salisbury the Beira Railway again placed orders for big engines with Neilson Reid of Glasgow. This time, however, they purchased four large 4–8–0s and followed this up with another twelve in 1900. These sturdy engines were much liked by the engineers and were used on a variety of lines throughout South Africa. Indeed, until 1905 this Seventh Class loco provided the power for nearly all the trains on the main lines, including Beira, Bulawayo and Vryburg to Victoria Falls.

At this time the main traffic flow was inland, as the area was part of an expanding economy. Besides taking passengers around the districts, trains were often loaded with construction materials. These engines now demonstrated their worth. On the Beira Railway they proved their abilities by managing to pull seven or eight loaded wagons, weighing between 210 and 240 tons. Part of the journey – the section of line between Bamboo Creek and Umtali – included a one in thirty-eight gradient with five chain curves. On the one in eighty gradients on to Bulawayo these locos could manage 400 tons. This in fact was not the end for some of these Seventh class engines. The outbreak of the first world war meant that more shunting engines were needed. But because supplies were rationed and difficult to obtain, it was decided to convert some of these old campaigners to tank engines. Two types were produced by extending their wheel frames from 4–8–0 to 4–8–2 and 4–8–4 arrangements. Provided with side tanks holding around 480 gallons, a further bunker tank for 500–650 gallons and a coal bunker capable of holding at most $4\frac{1}{2}$ tons, they were a rather different spectacle. Nine of the 4–8–2s were built and six 4–8–4s. They were a

Above A powerful GMA class Garratt climbs the steep gradient to the Montague Pass on the Port Elizabeth–Cape Town line.

Left A British-built South African Railways class 15F heads a freight at Dikgale in the Northern Transvaal.

Above A lightweight class 24 locomotive crosses the spectacular Kaaimans River Bridge on the branch line from Knysna to George, Cape Province.

Right A Rhodesia Railways 12th class at Bulawayo in 1975. These engines have now been largely superseded by the Garratts, but the type was widely used in Southern Africa for many years.

successful conversion and ran for a very long time – the last was
scrapped as late as 1956.

With the growing development of British possessions, and
increasing travel by the expanding population, it was realized that
new locomotive stock was needed, especially for the hilly sections of
line like those between Mafeking and Bulawayo. A new mountain
type of engine was ordered. Seven 4–8–2s with separate tenders
were bought from the North British Railway Company, based in
Glasgow. On arrival in South Africa these were designated Tenth
class. They were superheated engines with an attractive appearance; they were popular and, for their time, quite fast. They
were easily powerful enough to deal with the steeper gradients on
these lines and did much to reduce bottlenecks. The improved
timings evident from the Rhodesian timetables for 1931–3 owed
much to their smooth and efficient running. They continued in

Two powerful South African Railways locomotives 16E (left) and 15E (right) photographed at Bloemfontein in 1970.

service until 1961 when they were sent for scrap. In 1917 it was realized that an even more powerful mountain loco was required, and orders for a 4–8–2 class were placed with the Montreal Loco Works in Canada. These were called Eleventh class. Bigger still, they were designed to run at slower speeds but to haul heavier weights. They were used extensively for freight traffic and particularly for long coal trains, and later as the Rhodesian copper mines were opened up they were called on to work there.

In the mid-1920s pressure was again put upon the railway engineers to provide improved locos to deal with the increased traffic and demands for a more efficient service. The Twelfth class, a 4–8–2, was ordered for general passenger duties while the demand for a more powerful mountain loco was answered by the now famous Beyer Peacock Garratts. This distinctive class of engine was evolved from the ideas of the English engineer H. W. Garratt in collaboration with the builders Beyer Peacock in 1909. It consisted of a central boiler mounted by pivots at either end on to two separate engine units. Since the boiler and firebox were not above the wheels, their size was limited only by the loading gauge; for the same reason, wheels and cylinders could be made to any convenient diameter.

Twelve Garratts were ordered by Rhodesian Railways in 1925, and were called Thirteenth class. They had a wheel arrangement of 2–6–2 + 2–6–2. They were the forerunners of a fleet which was then expanded up to 250, and has become one of the distinctive features of Rhodesian Railways. Throughout the 1930s these locomotives were consistently re-ordered, with modifications. As time passed the Garratt designs became progressively bigger; other modifications included streamlining the water tank mounted over the front set of wheels. During the second world war the demand for essential raw materials from Africa was so great that the War Department provided new 2–8–2 + 2–8–2 Garratts for railways in Rhodesia, the Gold Coast and elsewhere. In Rhodesia these became the Eighteenth class. In 1949 Rhodesian Railways purchased ten Garratts from Sudan Railways; these were of an uncommon 4–6–4 + 4–6–4 arrangement. The final development of this locomotive design in Rhodesia came in 1953 when the RR's largest Garratts yet were ordered. These were the massive Twentieth and Twenty A class 4–8–2 + 2–8–4s, weighing some 223 tons and producing a tractive effort of 69,300 lb. Because of their size the fireman was provided with a mechanical stoker. They were largely used to haul coal trains from Wankie to Bulawayo with loads of 1800 tons.

The development of Beyer Garratt locomotives in Rhodesia which has been outlined here is just one example of how these locomotives have been adopted by the railways of many African countries. It has many parallels, notably in South Africa and Kenya. The Fifty-nine class Garratts of East African Railways are the largest steam locomotives still at work anywhere.

13 The Great Trains Revived

Although the age of steam has passed for nearly all of the world's major railway systems, the age of the great trains has not disappeared. The luxury expresses of modern Europe, connecting major cities separated by hundreds of miles in a few hours, offer a service that could not be matched even in the zenith of the age of steam. In Britain electrification and the advent of the high-speed train have transformed travel time.

For the railway enthusiast, however, the real enchantment of the great trains lay not in speed or comfort alone, but in the romance and excitement of steam. Steam had an attraction and an allure that could never be rivalled. It is this which has led to one of the most successful and popular leisure phenomena of post-war history – the rise of steam trains as a tourist attraction and of railway preservation societies dedicated to restoring the lost age of steam. In many countries the great trains of yesteryear have been re-created for the enjoyment of present and future generations.

In the USA an example of the steam revival has been seen on the Arcade and Attica Railroad. The line itself has a complex but fascinating history. It dates back to 1852 when a company was formed under the title Attica and Allegheny Valley Railroad to build a narrow-gauge line from Attica, New York, southwards for 75 miles to the state boundary between Pennsylvania and New York state. Some preliminary diggings were undertaken, but the project was abandoned in 1856. In February 1870 a second attempt was made and the Attica and Arcade Railroad Company was formed. However, after much further work the line was abandoned again. In 1880 a new company was formed, called the Tonawanda Valley Railroad Company; it planned to build a narrow-gauge line between Attica and Buffalo. By September 1880 19 miles had been completed,

Opposite above The Keighley and Worth Valley Railway, Yorkshire. A Stanier Black Five climbs the steep gradient out of Keighley towards the village of Oxenhope in the Pennine Hills.

Opposite below The Green Mountain Railway at Bellows Falls, Vermont. A former Canadian Pacific locomotive heads one of the regular tourist trains run during the summer months from Bellows Falls, which also boasts a large steam railway museum.

Above A Canadian Pacific locomotive, subsequently used by the Canmore Mines, and now one of the few operating steam locomotives in Canada. It is seen here at Heritage Park, Alberta.

Opposite A striking view of a Denver and Rio Grande Western locomotive at Silverton, Colorado.

on which trains were operating between Attica and Curriers. Yet the scheme as it was originally conceived was never completed and a line from Curriers to Arcade was laid. This was opened in May 1881. The company continued operating, but with diminishing success after the second world war.

It was in August 1962 that the railway decided to start using steam engines again. Although the idea took some time to catch on the prospect of a steam passenger railway caught people's imagination and the line has since prospered. But steam is not the only tourist attraction of the line. One of the company's coaches is of particular interest. This is the twelve-wheeled saloon named Warwick, painted in the green livery of the New York, Ontario and Western Railway Company; it was used to convey several illustrious passengers. It was built in 1886 when it was used by President Grover Cleveland to convey him and his wife on their honeymoon; later, in 1928, it was used by Alfred Smith, governor of New York, in his whistle-stop tour of the country in his bid for the presidency. The coach's fittings are by no means those of the conventional carriage, for it contains sleeping, observation and dining sections as well as quarters for a detective and valet and a small kitchen. It is now permanently sited at Arcade.

The Arcade and Attica is one of many tourist railroads in the USA. Some, like the A and A, are old-established common carrier railroads which have found in steam tourist trains a useful way of supplementing or even replacing regular income, and others have been built new as tourist attractions or preservation ventures.

A vintage locomotive and carriages photographed just south of Launceston during preparations for the Tasmanian Government Railway centenary celebrations in 1970.

One of the best known is the Silverton train, which is one of the world's great trains by any standard. It runs over the Silverton branch of the Denver and Rio Grande Western RR, the system's sole remaining 3-ft gauge section, and one which is now isolated from the rest of the railroad since the connecting line has been closed. The 45-mile branch from Durango to Silverton was built in 1882, in the remarkably short time of nine months and five days. The builders laboured through winter blizzards in the mountains of Colorado, and it is estimated that subsequently over 300 million dollars' worth of precious metals were carried over the line. The branch has had a passenger service since it opened, though it had declined to a thrice-weekly mixed train before the tourist boom. Now there are two passenger trains daily throughout the summer, each of which carries on average 460 passengers. The scenery is remarkable: high mountains, deep gorges, steep canyons, forests, waterfalls and rushing rivers.

The scenery on the Strasburg Railroad in Pennsylvania is less spectacular, being rolling farmland. But this 4½-mile line is the USA's oldest short line, and was founded in 1832. By the late 1950s it had fallen on hard times and abandonment was imminent when

One of two steam locomotives preserved
by the Swiss Rhaetian alpine railway
heads an excursion train in 1970.

some rail fans led by Henry K. Long raised sufficient funds to
purchase it. Their plan was to preserve the railroad and restore it by
operating it as a hobby. Steam locomotives, they found, were an
essential ingredient to attract the public (the Strasburg RR had gone
over to internal combustion many years before), and with steam
locomotives reintroduced and old passenger cars purchased and
restored, the railroad has become an attractive and busy line.

In 1946 Ellis D. Atwood built a 5½-mile railway round his
cranberry farm near South Carver, Massachusetts; and the
Edaville RR (so called after his initials) was no ordinary line.
Atwood had been able to purchase surviving locomotives and
rolling stock from closed 2-ft gauge railroads in Maine which he had
known during the thirties when they were still running. Several
such lines had served that state – they hauled timber, general
freight and passenger traffic and a great many people on vacation.
Their diminutive trains came to be regarded with affection.
Unfortunately this was not enough to overcome the depression
and motor competition, and during the 1930s and 1940s all were
closed. Atwood re-created a Maine 2-ft gauge line in Massachusetts
for his own enjoyment, but soon, when he found that crowds were

coming of their own accord to see his railroad, introduced a passenger train service. It was a great success. Now, some thirty years later, the Edaville RR continues to be busy, and a great many tourists come to travel on trains which narrowly escaped going for scrap thirty-five years ago.

In Australia, the Puffing Billy Preservation Society has ensured preservation of the train affectionately known as Puffing Billy. This runs on the surviving part of a 2 ft-6 ins gauge line in Victoria. In 1893 there was a big land boom in Victoria which soon burst, causing great financial distress and throwing thousands out of work as businesses dried up. The government was then based at Melbourne and it was clear that emergency measures were necessary to avoid rioting. At that time the railway from Melbourne only extended as far as Upper Fern Tree Gully at the foot of the Blue Dandenong ranges. Consequently the pioneers who farmed these ranges had an arduous journey by horse-drawn cart down some 2000 feet to the railhead and so to Melbourne. To appease the demands of the unemployed and to make travel much easier the government decided to build a 2 ft-6 ins gauge railway from Upper Fern Tree Gully to Gembrook in the hills, a distance of some 18 miles.

The railway was completed and opened in December 1900 and was at once nicknamed the Puffing Billy Line because of its quaint little engines and rolling stock. As the tracks progressed up into the hills, settlers, able to buy this land cheaply, flocked from the capital to make new homes. Not only settlers rode the train, though. Many day excursionists came up from Melbourne for an outing in the hills. The names of the stations are particularly evocative and convey much of this narrow gauge line's quality and character – Menzies Creek, named after an old gold digger who struck it rich, Clematis, Emerald, Nobelius and Lakeside.

The line was blocked by a landslip in 1952 and was closed. But the *Sun* newspaper arranged to run free specials, for children to say goodbye to Puffing Billy, from Upper Fern Tree Gully to Belgrave, the station before the landslip. These were popular, and about this time the PBPS was formed to keep the little train running, by providing a financial guarantee and voluntary labour. In 1958 the track from Upper Fern Tree Gully to Belgrave was widened and electrified so that suburban trains from Melbourne could use it. The society took on the tremendous task of reopening the closed line from Belgrave as far as Lakeside, $8\frac{1}{4}$ miles, which meant re-laying much of the track and reinstating the railway past the landslip. The first section was reopened in 1962 but Lakeside was not reached until 1975. In the meantime Puffing Billy had gone on from strength to strength with additional locomotives and coaches being added to cope with the crowds. The locomotives are attractive 2–6–2Ts; though built in Australia, their appearance betrays the design's American origin, for the first two of the class were imported from Baldwin Locomotive Works, USA.

In Britain steam preservation lines have become immensely popular. The preservation movement first began to get under way after 1950. The first in the world was the Talyllyn Railway in Wales – a marvellous example of a working Victorian narrow-gauge railway. The death in 1950 of the owner of the Talyllyn, Sir Henry Haydn Jones, threatened the whole future of the railway. The idea of preservation gradually came to fruition. This was eventually achieved by a voluntary society that took over the railway. Whit Monday 1951 saw the first public train in the world operated by a preservation society, when the locomotive *Dolgoch* pulled out of Towyn hauling it. Since then, other narrow-gauge lines in Wales, such as the Festiniog, have been revived by enthusiastic pre-servation societies. It was formerly a slate-carrying line which had literally to be dug out by volunteers after vegetation had clogged the line after eight years of disuse. The 'great little trains' of Wales are now highly-popular tourist attractions.

The honour of being the first standard-gauge line in Britain to be operated by preservationists belongs to the Middleton Railway in Leeds, where a freight service was begun in 1960. In the same year, one of the most popular of all the preserved railways began operation – the Bluebell Railway in Sussex. Established in 1960 as a living museum for the steam train in a rural branch-line setting, it has become one of the major attractions of south-eastern England. From small beginnings with two locomotives and two coaches, the Bluebell Railway is now the home of the largest and most comprehensive collection of vintage railway locomotives that operated in the south of England. Situated in the heart of the Sussex Weald and running for 5 miles through some of its most beautiful countryside, the line offers an ideal setting for operating vintage steam trains. The stations and equipment too are also of interest, since they date from the construction of the line in 1882. At Sheffield Park, at the southern end of the line, the pre-1923 atmosphere of the London, Brighton and South Coast Railway is still strong, with oil-lit platform lamps. Slowly restoration work has been put in hand to make the atmosphere more accurate and complete. At Horsted Keynes at the north end of the line the emphasis is on the period immediately following 1923 when the Southern Railway had taken over. The railway collection includes a stud of about sixteen vintage steam locomotives which show some of the main develop-ments in steam locomotive design from 1872 to 1951. Among the oldest locomotives from the former London, Brighton and South Coast Railway are Nos. 55 *Stepney* and 72 *Fenchurch*, built at Brighton Works in 1875 and 1872 respectively by William Stroudley; No. 72 celebrated its centenary in 1972, being the oldest working standard gauge locomotive in the country. Two locos from the old LSWR are locomotive No. 488, one of the famous Adams radial tank locomotives built in 1885, most of which disappeared in the 1920s, and Adams dock tank No. 96. The Southern Railway itself

The Talyllyn Railway, North Wales, the first centre for British preserved steam and a fine example of a Victorian narrow gauge railway.

is represented by *Blackmore Vale,* one of the West Country class locomotives mentioned in Chapter 4, and USA Dock Tank 30064. The atmosphere of the great trains is recaptured even more authentically by Maunsell coaches of the 1930s and by post-war Bulleid main-line coaches.

Not surprisingly enthusiasts of the Great Western, with its unique place in Britain's railway history, have also played a prominent part in this revival of the great trains. Early in 1961 the 48xx Preservation Society was born with the main intention of preserving a 14xx (ex-48xx) auto-train engine and trailer coach. Progress was slow initially until the first milestone was reached in March 1964 when locomotive 1466 was purchased. Even before this time the name of the society had been changed to Great Western Society to reflect a broadening interest in all things Great Western. In mid-1965 a fund was started to preserve a two-cylinder 4–6–0 locomotive, and the response was so successful that by early 1966 the society had taken delivery of 6998 *Burton Agnes Hall.* From this time the collection began to grow steadily, with the purchase by the society's Bristol group of 0–6–2T 6697 and acquisition by members of 6106 and 7808 *Cookham Manor.* In 1967 a different opportunity arose for the society. The locomotive depot at Didcot in Oxfordshire ceased to be used by British Rail and it was offered to the society. Since then the society has not looked back. At first there were four engines and half-a-dozen carriages: now there are seventeen engines displaying a complete cross-section of latter-day Great Western locomotive power, including Castle class 4–6–0s *Earl Bathurst* and *Nunney,* Hall class 4–6–0s *Burton Agnes Hall, Hinderton Hall* and *Maindy Hall,* Manor class 4–6–0 *Cookham Manor,* and a variety of smaller engines. Some have been fully restored to working order and repainted in original livery, whilst others recently rescued from the scrapyard still await attention. There are now fifteen modern GWR carriages, including two of the sumptuous Ocean Saloons, and

a number of vintage four-wheeled and clerestory carriages dating
from the turn of the century. Didcot is ideally placed for running
steam excursions over British Rail lines. The Great Western
Society's own 6998 *Burton Agnes Hall* has made trips to Birmingham, Hereford and Stratford-on-Avon, while engines from other
depots have visited Didcot, amongst them such famous engines as
No. 4472 *Flying Scotsman*, No. 4498 *Sir Nigel Gresley*, No. 4471
Green Arrow and No. 7029 *Clun Castle* (a fine example of the
powerful Castle class locomotives).

Also in the Great Western domain are two delightful Devon
branch lines that have been revived – the Dart Valley Railway and
the Torbay Steam Railway. Both railways run for a considerable
distance alongside the beautiful river Dart. The Dart Valley
Railway was re-opened in 1969 after being closed to all traffic since
1962. The main station is at Buckfastleigh, where the railway's
rolling stock is mainly kept. Here, one can also see work going on
towards restoring engines and carriages. The line wends its way
towards Totnes, hugging the river bank for much of the way.
Staverton Bridge is one of those timeless wayside country stations
which is a joy to behold. The Torbay Steam Railway was taken over
direct from BR and came into its new ownership on 1 January 1973. It
is a breathtaking route overlooking Torbay and the beaches at
Goodrington and Broadsands. There are high viaducts, deep
cuttings and a long tunnel, then the wonderful approach to
Kingswear where the line runs alongside the river Dart, full of

boats of all sizes from dinghies to schooners, and frigates at anchor near the Britannia Royal Naval College at Dartmouth.

Much steam revival has also taken place outside the Great Western, not least in Yorkshire and the north-west. In Yorkshire, the Keighley and Worth Valley Railway has marvellously re-created a bygone age. The railway was once a British Railways branch line, but it has been operated since 1968 by a private limited company under the auspices of a railway preservation society. Trains are operated every Saturday, Sunday and Bank Holiday throughout the year, and there are extensive midweek services during parts of July and August. During the 5-mile journey from the mill town of Keighley to the village of Oxenhope, which is surrounded by the Pennine hills, the train climbs 330-ft up an average gradient of one in seventy-six, a challenge for any steam engine. The locomotive and carriage collection is kept at Oxenhope (where there is a large display shed) and Haworth (the workshops). There are over thirty engines here – one of the largest private collections in the north. Part of the appeal of the Worth Valley railway lies in its scenery and history. Haworth village has long been a tourist attraction because it is the home of the Brontë family, and has become an established literary shrine. The Brontë parsonage museum is open daily and attracts visitors from all over the world. Miles of unspoilt moorland stretch in all directions around Haworth offering magnificent views.

Another important steam venture is the Steamtown Railway Museum at Carnforth. The motive power depot at Carnforth was one of the last in the country to retain steam locomotives. After the final withdrawal of steam motive power in 1968, a private company promoted by a number of steam enthusiasts leased the depot in order to house various locomotives which had been bought for preservation. The leased area covers about 37 acres and in addition to the shed, offices and workshops it contains a coaling tower, ash disposal plant, water columns, a 70-ft turntable and a carriage and wagon shop. From end to end the site is about a mile long and has approximately 4 miles of track. The southern end lies on the west side of the main line from London to Glasgow, now electrified. A rail connection at the northern end allows access to and from the Furness line of British Rail. There are over thirty British and continental main-line and industrial locos on view.

The dream of many enthusiasts was not to re-create the great trains of yesteryear simply as static exhibits, or confined to relatively tiny branch lines, but to take over for steam a section of a former main line. In 1969 the Main Line Preservation Group was formed to acquire 'a suitable length of main line for the operation of steam-hauled passenger trains at realistic speeds'.

This group later became the Main Line Steam Trust Limited and concentrated its efforts on several miles of the Great Central Railway main line between Loughborough, Leicestershire, which

Opposite above A former Great Western locomotive at Buckfastleigh Station on the Dart Valley Railway, South Devon, a line re-opened by railway enthusiasts in 1969.

Opposite below Five beautifully preserved locomotives on display at the Steamtown Railway Museum at Carnforth, Lancashire. On the extreme right is *Hardwicke*, veteran of the 1895 race to Aberdeen, and on its left 4472 *Flying Scotsman*.

had been recently closed by British Rail. The $3\frac{3}{4}$ -acre site of Loughborough central station was leased by the trust and became the base of operations. The Great Central Railway was the last main line to be built in Great Britain and there were many who considered it unnecessary. But its promoters' optimism was justified, and after its route was opened to passengers in March 1899 the new railway soon gained a well deserved reputation for fast, comfortable and frequent express trains. It continued to serve as a main-line trunk route for over sixty years and in its heyday boasted named expresses such as the South Yorkshireman and the Master Cutler. During the 1960s the line was gradually run down until only a limited local service out of Marylebone and between Rugby and Nottingham remained. The latter was finally closed and abandoned on 5 May 1969. The railway had been superbly engineered with no steep gradients and with broad curves to provide no hindrance to speeding locomotives. There are no level crossings and the line crosses picturesque Leicestershire hunting and farming country.

Despite the valiant efforts of the steam preservationists, the sights and smells of the era of the Great Trains have now all but vanished. Over a century and a half has gone by since the age of steam dawned on the world. Now that age has passed. No more do the steam giants of the Union Pacific or Canadian Pacific battle with the vast distances and gruelling gradients of the North American mountains and prairies. The Anglo-Scottish expresses no longer attack Beattock and Shap Summit in a fury of steam on their 'Race to the North'. The shrill whistle of a Gresley Pacific racing down Stoke bank disturbs no more the quiet peace of rural England.

All that remains of the era of steam are the more enduring memorials of a lost age – the great engineering feats, the viaducts and bridges, the tunnels and vast stretches of seemingly interminable track, and perhaps most nostalgic of all, the stations. In London, elegant Paddington, busy Victoria, and even St Pancras, with its Gothic splendour, remain as memorials – but the glistening steam locos that gave them their life have disappeared.

Elsewhere, the famous expresses still remain – some, like the TEEs, offering a comfort and speed unrivalled in the age of steam. But the magic has gone. The Orient Express has lost its air of mystery. The romance has vanished from the great trans-continental journeys across Australia and Canada. The 'Great Trains' gave to the nineteenth-century world not only a new concept in luxury travel and ostentatious comfort, but also the special enchantment which lay in faraway names on their destination boards. Now, with the advent of 'jet-set' travel, even the once romantic names of Constantinople or the Côte d'Azur have lost their special appeal. The legacy of the 'Great Trains', however, will always remain. The coming of the railways changed the course of history, and now, in turn, the changing course of history has brought to an end the great railway era.

Acknowledgments

The author and publishers would like to express their thanks to P.J.G.Ransom and Edgar Jones for their help in the preparation of this book. They also wish to thank all those who have provided photographs and in particular P. B. Whitehouse for his assistance.
The photographs and illustrations are reproduced by kind permission of the individuals and organisations listed below. Photographers' names are given in italics and where they did not personally supply the pictures their names appear in brackets. The page numbers of colour photographs are given in italics.

Australian National Railways *113* below; Australian News and Information Bureau 104, 107, 111; The Bluebell Railway 137; British Museum (Fotomas) 46 above and below, 58; British Rail-Oxford Publishing Company 15; Canadian Pacific 95, *96*, 99; Colourviews Picture Library *25* above (*P.M.Alexander*), *25* below (*P.B.Whitehouse*), *42* (*D.Cross*), *50* (French Railways), *61* (*P.B.Whitehouse*), *88* above and *89* (*J.M.Jarvis*), *93* (*Peter Howard*), 114, *121* (*P.B.Whitehouse*), 123, *125* below (*C.M. Whitehouse*), 126, 127 (*Charles Lewis*), *128* below (*P.B.Whitehouse*), 130 (*C.M.Whitehouse*), 133 (*P.B.Whitehouse*), 139 above (*J.M.Boyes*); Compagnie Internationale des Wagons-Lits 47 above, right and below, 54 above and below, 59, 63 left and right; William H. Coverdale Collection *84, 85* below; *D.Cross* 28 above *113* above; Deutschesbahn Zentrales Bildarchiv 51 above; *F.Dumbleton* 28 below; East African Railways Commission 122; Elek Books 9; Mary Evans Picture Library 49, 56, 98, 119 below; *C.Gammell* 24, *29, 120* left, *128* above, 136; German Federal Railways 51 below; *Victor Goldberg 85* above; Hamlyn Books (Union Pacific Railroad) 90; *Victor Hands 92*; Illinois Central Railroad endpapers; Keystone Press 131; Mansell Collection 2–3, 10, 11, 12; New English Library (*B. Sharpe*) 17, 26, *32*; New South Wales Department of Railways 103; Popperfoto 23 above, 60, 67 above, 73 above; Popperfoto-Colourviews Picture Library 22 (*P.F.Bowles*), 23 (*G.F.Heiron*), 35 above (*Eric Treacy*), 40 (*J.F.Ashman*), 41 (*C.M.Whitehouse*), 45 (*P.M.Alexander*), 53 (Austrian Federal Railways), *88* below (*P.B.Whitehouse*); Public Archives of Canada 100; Radio Times Hulton Picture Library 34, 35 below, 36, 44, 76, 79, 118, 119 above; Rail Transport Commission of New South Wales 110; *D.Rodgers 116–17, 124* above and below, *125* above; Santa Fe Railways 83, Science Museum, London 6, 8; Snark International *20–21*, 67 below; Swiss National Tourist Office 52; Steamtown Railway Museum, Carnforth 139 below; Thamesdown Museums, Swindon 16; Union Pacific Railroad 70, 73 below, *74, 81*; La Vie du Rail 64.

The publishers also wish to thank Constable & Co for kind permission to quote from *Reminiscences* by R.E.Crompton.

Glossary

Table of British and American Railway Terms

BRITAIN	USA
bank	grade
bogie	truck
carriage	passenger car
chimney	smoke stack
coupling	coupler
cowcatcher	pilot
drawbar	draft iron
driver	engineman
fireman	stoker
footplate	deck
guard	conductor
guard's van	caboose
luggage van	baggage car
marshalling yard	classifying yard
railway	railroad
regulator	throttle
shunt	switch
signal box	tower
signal gantry	gallery
sleeper	tie
van	box car
wagon	freight car

Index

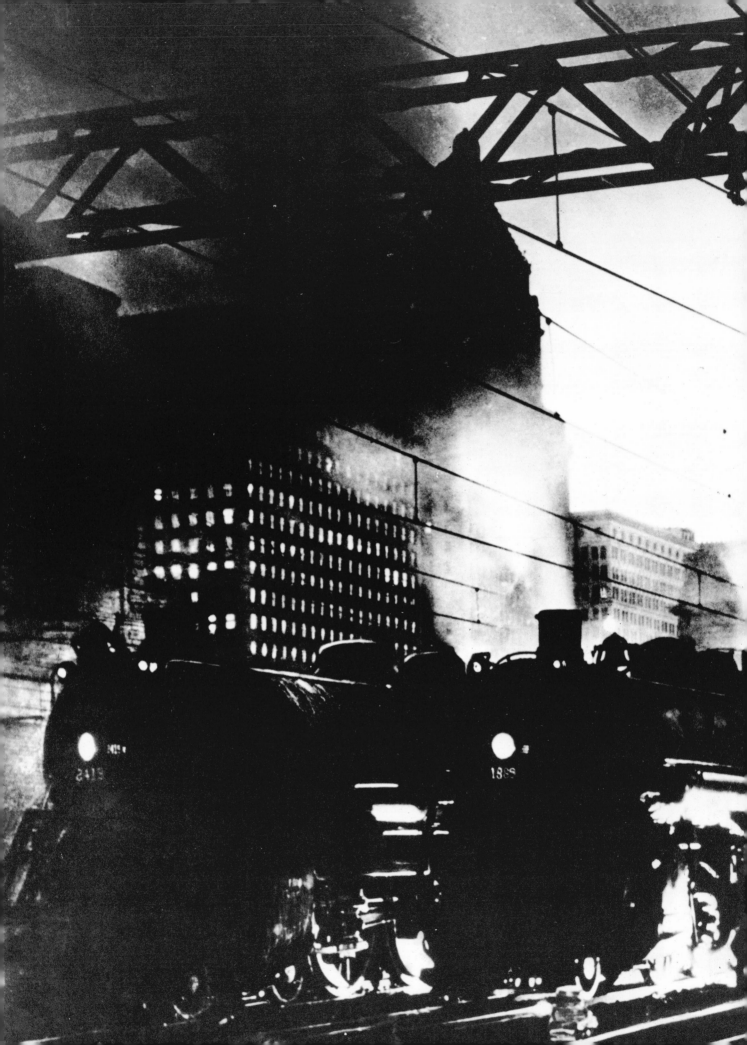